LIVING
WITHOUT
REGRETS

6 ESSENTIAL KEYS
TO PERSONAL FREEDOM

Linda:
It is an honor
to know you & call
you "friend". May God
richly bless you as you
lead others to their journey
of freedom....
Cinda McGregor

A Story of Challenge, Triumph, Bravery, and Persistence

LIVING WITHOUT REGRETS

6 ESSENTIAL KEYS
TO PERSONAL FREEDOM

Survivor of Terminal Ovarian Cancer
CINDA M. GREGORY

LIVING WITHOUT REGRETS
6 ESSENTIAL KEYS TO PERSONAL FREEDOM

ISBN (Print Edition): 978-1-7333853-0-5

ISBN (Kindle Version): 978-1-7333853-1-2

Library of Congress Control Number (LCCN): 2019911020

Printed in the United States of America

Published by Cinda M. Gregory, Sherburne, NY | www.willgohere.com

Prepared for publication by Wendy K. Walters | www.wendykwalters.com

To contact the author: cindamgregory@gmail.com

PRAISE FOR LIVING WITHOUT REGRETS

For anyone who has made mistakes in the past and is still struggling with the associated guilt and regret, *Living Without Regrets* is a great book. Cinda does a great job of illustrating powerful biblical principles leading to freedom through her own life's journey. I have known Bob and Cinda for over a decade, and their faith and perseverance in the face of a terminal ovarian cancer diagnosis has been an incredible inspiration to all who know them. I highly recommend Cinda's book to you. As you read it, you'll learn the specific keys necessary to live the rest of your life with no regrets for the past, and great hope and faith for the future.

—CRAIG HILLl

Founder, Family Foundations International
Author of over 20 books including *The Power of a Parent's Blessing*
www.craighill.org

Cinda Gregory's gripping book, *Living Without Regrets,* provides essential keys to personal freedom. Her ability to share vulnerably and articulate matters of the heart are life giving and refreshing. Barriers to healing are gently addressed in a way that makes the reader feel safe. Her life is a living epistle of a life well lived. If the greatest desire of your heart is to become whole and live a vibrant life, this book is a must read. Keys to freedom are found from the opening statements through her gripping testimony of wounding to wholeness. *"To appoint unto them that mourn in Zion, to give unto them beauty for ashes, the oil of joy for mourning, the garment of praise for the spirit of heaviness; that they might be called trees of righteousness, the planting of the Lord, that he might be glorified"* (Isaiah 61:3, KJV).

—MAUREEN GRAHAM

Psychiatric Mental Health Nurse, Nurse Practitioner, Adult Nurse Practitioner

This life we live can be riddled with painful, negative experiences. Stuffing it away for another day only invites turmoil within oneself that eventually surfaces when least expected. With unashamed truth, Cinda Gregory shares the candid reality of significant choices there were key in her life journey of *Living Without Regrets*. Once you read the introduction you won't want to put the book down!

JOHN AND KRISTY CAMP

Senior Pastors, Resurrection Life Fellowship
Madison, NY

Cinda Gregory is a woman of courage and strength. In *Living Without Regrets,* Cinda gives the reader a glimpse into the source of her bravery and tenacity. As you embark on this journey with Cinda you can actually receive an impartation from her wisdom as she practically guides us into the realm of the supernatural. We may not know how to get there, but Cinda skillfully weaves a story of challenge and triumph, bravery and persistence that leads to the reward of peace. This is a peace that guards our heart and imparts a sense of well-being that God Himself is holding your life. Cinda is a skilled writer who powerfully weaves eternal truths into her story, while imparting hope to the reader. In her earnest style she gently explores the powerful reality of abundant life even in the midst of life's storm. Cinda is a powerfully loving woman whose faith in God is an inspiration to all who know her. She is unwilling to settle for anything but God's purpose for her life. As you read you will be encouraged to live your life without regrets!"

KARREN TURNER

Co-founder of Lions Gate Ministries
Author of *Freedom from the Victim Mindset*

I have known Bob and Cinda for 33 years and have firsthand witnessed God's marvelous transformation in their lives. I've seen them walk from dysfunction to function, to freedom, to facilitating free-dom in the lives of so many. Their victorious walk through some deep struggles proves there's a God in heaven who cares! Within the pages of *Living Without Regrets* are nuggets of truth and life wisdom that can guide your transformation to find God's place of freedom He intended for you. If you are hopeless about your life, marriage or health, then you need to read this book!

AL CHANDLER
Senior Pastor, Randallsville New Life Church
Randallsville, NY

Trauma. Truth. Perseverance. Freedom. Four words to encapsulate the human journey. In this transparent and vulnerable book, Cinda lays out principles she has learned in her Christian walk to bring freedom to the hard places in life. Trauma happens to us all. Facing the truth and pain of trauma instead of denying its power in us, brings us to a point of decision. Will we persevere through the pain, applying God's prescription for your freedom? Apply to your life what Cinda has learned, letting God restore the broken in you to beauty that lights the way for others."

LINDA FORSTER,
Founder and Director of Healing the Heart Ministries
Author, titles including: *Forgiveness: Gateway to Healing, Unmasking the Great Pretender: Breaking Bonds of Shame, Living Free!*

We have known Cinda for almost 20 years, and grew to love her and her husband as we worked together in ministry to marriages. Her candid writing style will encourage you to keep pressing on for God's best in your own life, and her passionate heart will draw you into her story ... and maybe even encourage you to write your own!

JIM AND EVA JOHNSON

Former Regional Directors for Marriage Ministries International
Directors of Marriage Ministry at Sonrise Christian Center
Everett, WA

Cinda Gregory's transparency concerning her thoughts and feelings will be a great benefit to anyone that reads *Living Without Regrets*. She shares her fears and faith openly and truthfully as she expresses her "What-if" thoughts that most assuredly would be shared by a person diagnosed with a life limiting illness. Candidly sharing her faith walk and desire to finish well would definitely encourage anyone who desires to hear God say, "Well done good and faithful servant." If you need encouragement to live on in faith and victory, *Living Without Regrets* is a must read!"

JERRY SALIBA

Former Senior Pastor Randallsville New Life Church
Pastor Emeritus, Randallsville New Life Church
Randallsville, NY

Cinda's writing gift is her willingness to share her raw reality of life-experiences with us. Through her stories you can catch a glimpse of a God that restores and rebuilds lives. Each of us can receive His gift of replication, if we simply consent to a "trade up." Her prayers at the end of each chapter provide the tools to achieve freedom, available to each of us through the blood of Jesus. Thank you, Cinda, for exposing your life so others can experience "cage free" living!

WENDY SHEPARD
Program Director & Clinical Nurse Specialist at John Hopkins
Bayview, Baltimore, MD
Ministry Team Leader at Life Center Ministries
Harrisburg, PA
Prayer Minister for Healing the Hearts Ministry.

Cinda Gregory is a true spiritual mother in every sense of the word. She exudes passion to see others around her set free and she does this from experience. She knows freedom and wants you to know it too. You will find *Living Without Regrets* to be an intentional, raw, and powerful dive into the realm of true freedom through Christ. Coming to you like a stealth ninja, this book will open your heart to the reality of the world around you while giving power to the source within—true freedom in Jesus. *Living Without Regrets* is a must read if you long for freedom and intention in your life!"

MARK AND KATIE MONROE
Pastors of Lighthouse Community Church
Earlville, NY

Raw, unvarnished truth presented with an enormous dose of hope... is an apt description of Cinda's debut book. With candor and vulnerability, she challenges readers to reject the schemes of the enemy which obstruct the path to freedom and to embrace the fullness of a life lived without the weight of fear and guilt. Whether you're the one ready to embark upon the journey of deep, personal healing to discover how Jesus can rewrite your story or you know someone who is, this book will be a valuable resource in that quest!"

PEGGY PARDOE

B.S.N.
Prayer Minister, *Covenant of Peace Ministries*
Facilitator, *Family Foundations International*
Harrisburg, PA

DEDICATION

I dedicate this book to my father, Richard E. Molyneaux (1919-2017). He taught me how to live well, and then in his golden years, taught me how to die well. He had an insatiable love for life, was endlessly optimistic, and truly enjoyed people!

Dad, you were (and still are) my hero. Thank you for always loving me, encouraging me, and being proud of me. Even before I came to know my Heavenly Father, I knew what it was to be the "apple" of my father's eye.

ACKNOWLEDGMENTS

The writing of this book has most definitely been a team effort. My editors: Sue Pincofski, Michelle Smith, Peggy Pardoe, Sarah Gregory, and Denise Rainville helped me create something that was so much better than I could have ever done on my own! Sue, you understood my heart and what I was saying. You worked your magic to put such a beautiful edge on my stories! Peggy and Michelle, you are gifted as "Word-Smiths"! Thank you for your valuable contributions. Sarah, you took a very rough draft of my manuscript and helped me see the direction I wanted to go and the vulnerability I wanted to tell it with! Thank you. Denise, your expertise with grammar and sentence structure was a huge blessing.

I want to thank my loving husband, Bob, and my three wonderful daughters Sarah, Jamie, and April for allowing me to write this book and tell the stories with vulnerability and transparency. I love you forever.

There were many others that encouraged me to tell my story and persevere to the completion of the project: Wes and Beth Tuthill, Lisa Collins, Deb Foster, Rebecca and Earl Nussbaum, Maryanne Sykes, Peggy Pardoe, Wendy Shepard, Gale Chapple, Linda Diamond, Beth Krug, Steve and Melissa Trass, Elizabeth Thallinger, Mike and Joanne Moore, Erma and Sam Martin, Steve and Kathleen Zimmerman, Wendy Chapura, Carl Ohlson, Melissa Bogert and my father Richard E. Molyneaux. You helped bring a dream to a reality!

Last but absolutely not least, I want to thank my Heavenly Father. He has been the constant in my life—the One who never leaves me nor forsakes me—the one who is always encouraging me to be my very best!

CONTENTS

INTRODUCTION
HOW IT ALL BEGAN

"The issue is not simply how long you have to run or how well you have to run, but how you have finished. Joab ran most of his race well, but then crashed near the finish line."

BOB SORGE

"What we believe determines the way we live our lives."

LOREN CUNNINGHAM AND DAVID JOEL HAMILTON

What if? What if you were suddenly informed that your life was nearing its end? Have you ever wondered how you would feel? Would you decide that you had lived your life well or be saddened with regrets? Perhaps we all think of such questions, but few of us admit to it. Every once in a while I had found my mind wandering to the land of *What-Ifs*. What if I had chosen a different career path? What if I had never exchanged wedding vows with Bob? What if we had never been blessed with three amazing daughters? Inevitably it would always come down to this... *what if I was told that I only had a short time to live?* How would I feel? What would fill me with regret? Having heard numerous stories of people who faced the end with an armload of misgivings over how they'd lived, led me to wonder how I would respond in their situation. Although my heart broke for them – they'd been robbed of any peace or hope – I did not want to find myself in that place. Was it even possible to believe that God would one day say to me, "Well done, thy good and faithful servant?" What must one do to truly finish well? Little did I know that in May 2014, at the age of 55, I would come face-to-face with death... transforming those musings into cold reality.

Bob and I had always prided ourselves in our lifestyle choices. We ate a healthy diet, exercised regularly, took good care of ourselves and felt young at heart. So when I felt a twinge on the left side of my pelvis, I didn't think much of it. When it persisted for a week, I made an appointment with my primary care provider. After numerous appointments, a battery of tests and subsequent phone calls, I found myself seated in the exam room of a gynecological surgeon. She was concerned as some of my blood work was out of the normal range and my enlarged ovary could be detected upon palpation. However, I looked healthy, felt normal and other than some discomfort on my left side, was still enjoying mountain biking. I simply never considered that it might be anything serious. I was wrong.

I had surgery the following week. The next morning my surgeon informed me that although the diagnosis was ovarian cancer—it appeared that my body had done a remarkable job in containing it. She emphasized that we needed to wait for the pathology results to know the full extent of what we were dealing with, yet we felt hopeful and optimistic because it had been caught early. Two weeks later, Bob and I met with the surgeon to discuss the results. Unexpectedly the cancer had metastasized from my pelvis, and was more advanced than originally believed. In addition, this particular form of ovarian cancer was "capillary serous," known to be very aggressive.

My husband and I were in shock. It didn't seem real. We cried. The surgeon cried. It was a terrifying dream that I couldn't wake up from. My first reaction was not to undergo chemotherapy as I felt that my body had already been assaulted enough! The surgeon urged me to reconsider. She felt certain that if I did not elect to undergo chemotherapy, I would not be alive to celebrate Christmas. I remember walking out of her office gripping Bob's arm, as I was still very weak. It felt as if we were trying to hold each other up. Dazed, we climbed into the car and headed for home. It certainly was not the report we had expected and hoped for!

On our way home, neither of us felt much like talking. We were literally in shock ... what could we say? Our home was over an hour away, so we had lots of time to think. All those years when I had casually and flippantly imagined *"what if,"* now here I was, here WE were, facing this as a REALITY! Wow! I started to ask myself, *"How do I feel?"* I didn't feel any of the emotions I has always imagined I would. Again, I asked myself the same question: *"How **do** I feel?"* I was shocked to realize that I felt at peace with the way I had lived my life and with the decisions I had made. I felt NO regrets! I couldn't believe it! Honestly, I had *never* thought this would be my response! Suddenly, and unexpectedly, I felt God speak to my heart and say, "You have finished well." Once again, I was shocked and overwhelmed because I had never expected that either. I spent the remainder of our ride in silence, mulling this over.

A few nights later, God woke me in the middle of the night to once again speak to my heart. "The reason you have no regrets is because of some critical choices you made at various times in your life. You did not necessarily see them as critical choices at the time, but that's what they were. You saw them as simple, almost insignificant choices. Get up and write them down because they did indeed change your life."

This book describes those critical decisions to which God referred and the experiences that resulted from them. Although I did not realize it at the time, each decision was an important key to freedom. They were simple, yet at the same time, very profound. They changed me and charted the course of my life. When I was forced to come face-to-face with death, these decisions had already produced such an abundance of spiritual fruit that I was able to agree with God: yes, I had finished well and without regret. The most exciting part is that if I did it, so can you! I invite you to join me on this journey to freedom so that one day you too may hear, "Well done, thy good and faithful servant."

FREEDOM
OUR CHOICE TO BE WHOLE

"Most people can look back and identify a time and place at which their lives changed significantly. Whether by accident or design, these are the moments when because of a readiness within us and a collaboration of events around us, we are forced to seriously reappraise ourselves and the conditions under which we live, and to make choices that will affect the rest of our lives."

FREDERIC F. FLACH

I grew up in the 1960s. As the sexual revolution and civil unrest were sweeping the nation, my family felt like "Leave it to Beaver." Like Harriet, my mom did not work outside the home, her main concern being our family; my dad was the breadwinner. As children, we didn't have a care in the world. My biggest concern was how I was going to entertain myself next. I thought our family was perfect. I felt very loved by my parents and many relatives. I had three siblings I adored. I was given the freedom to explore the world around me and had many child-sized adventures. My life had not yet crashed. Not yet hit the wall that would take me the next twenty-five years to recover from.

When I was young, we lived in a very small town. Many of our extended family members resided on the same street. I typically spent the days playing near my mom while she did her cleaning, sewing and whatever other tasks were involved in running the household. One day, while my mom was baking, a teenage boy who lived nearby came for a visit and engaged my mother in conversation. He was sixteen years old, and why he was not attending school as my two older siblings were is still a mystery. I was playing in an adjacent room with my dolls. When mom realized that she did not have enough butter to finish the cake, she asked him to keep an eye on me while she drove two blocks to the grocery store. It was fine with me as I was engrossed in an imaginary world with my dolls.

Soon after she'd left, he joined me in the room, and invited me to "play house" with him. I enthusiastically answered, "Yes!" because this was one of my favorite games. He then proceeded to explain **his** version of playing house. He would be the daddy, I would be the mommy and we would make babies. I distinctly remember feeling a chill run through my little body, a sense of warning. Something seemed "off" about what he was saying. Being so young, I was too naive to identify the problem. I do remember feeling terrified, yet also afraid to disagree with him. I wanted to keep playing—alone—with my dolls. He must have sensed my uneasiness, because he then began to reassure me that it would not only be okay, but really fun as well. I hesitantly agreed.

The grocery store was only a quarter of a mile away and my mother couldn't have been gone for more than ten minutes. She later told my father that while she was standing in the check-out line, she'd suddenly experienced an overwhelming sense that I was in danger. Somehow intuiting that she needed to get home right away, she dropped the butter and sprinted to her car.

Having defied the speed limit, she came flying through the door, straight to the room where I had been playing. There I was, lying on the floor, with my dress pulled up and my panties pulled down. The boy was already on top of me, about to penetrate. I was terrified, and I clearly remember feeling shame and guilt descend on me as I heard my mom scream, "HEY! WHAT'S GOING ON IN HERE?!" She raged like a mother bear, tearing into the boy and throwing him out of the house. She threatened his life if he ever dared touch me again.

THE SHROUD OF SHAME

Although my mother's angry question had not been directed at me, in the innocence of a four year-old, I took the responsibility upon my little girl self, along with the embarrassment and dirty feelings. A deep sense of shame filled me. It had to be my fault. After all, although I knew that somehow it was wrong, I had still agreed to play house with him. My mother didn't project this feeling onto me; it was an inside job. Of course, I could not articulate any of this as I was a mere child. The shame became a shroud that I secretly wrapped myself in. I lived under this darkness for the next twenty-five years. Was this feeling rational? No. Had anyone blamed me? Absolutely not. Yet, I could not silence the voice of self-condemnation. That attack shattered my young world and robbed me of my innocence.

These days, a mother confronted with the same situation would undoubtedly call the police. But this was over fifty years ago and "these things" were often kept secret, to be handled within the family. Soon afterward, my parents had convinced themselves that they'd dealt with the molestation and felt assured that this boy would no longer be a threat to their daughter. They essentially buried the violation. Neither of his parents nor anyone else outside of our immediate family were ever informed of his foiled rape attempt. Sadly, they would soon discover that their confidence was severely misplaced.

Call it naivete. Call it ignorance. Whatever you choose to call it, it was a huge mistake. I no longer recall how much time elapsed between his first rape attempt and his being allowed to periodically visit our house again. You see, he wasn't just a neighbor's son. He was my cousin! In retrospect, my parents imparted more grace than was warranted. I was now terrified by his presence and would do my best to stay close to my parents and siblings whenever he came near.

Not long afterward, my mom was once again preoccupied in the kitchen, and my cousin approached me as I was playing in our yard. His physical presence caused a wave of terror to crash over me. I quickly spun and ran toward the house ... to the safety of my mom. I bolted through the garage and headed toward the short breezeway that connected the garage to the kitchen. I quickly opened the outer breezeway door, leaving only a few steps between me and that kitchen door. Suddenly, with a sickening feeling, I realized that I did not hear the outer door fully close. Looking over my shoulder, I saw that he had followed me into the enclosed breezeway! Fear once again squeezed my young heart. As I tried to take another step toward the kitchen, he grabbed me. I couldn't scream; I couldn't utter a single word. I was terrified, frozen in my tracks. I adored dresses so I was once again wearing a frilly little number. Restraining me, he quickly pulled up my dress, stuck his hand down my panties and began to fondle me.

Once again God enabled my mother to come to my rescue. She later told me she had no idea that my cousin was on our property. She continued to explain how she perceived something was amiss. Apparently, when the outer door of the breezeway would open, the change in air pressure would cause the inner door (the one leading to the kitchen) to rattle slightly. This was an anomaly inherent to our house, one that my mom was aware of, but typically paid little attention to. That day, though, it did register in her subconscious that while the kitchen door had rattled, no one had come through it. She briefly ignored it, but was then filled with unmistakable deja vu ... *something was wrong!* Quickly opening the door, she once again discovered us together: me standing like a statue and him with his hand down my panties. To this day, I have no idea what she said or did to him. I was in that place AGAIN! In shock and overwhelmed by embarrassment, I remember none of what followed. Whatever transpired, my cousin never threatened me from that day forward and I don't remember him ever being in our house again.

I remember my parents feeling very blessed by the Divine intervention that had spoken through my mother's intuition, enabling her to "save" me from my perverted cousin. They felt relieved that disaster had once again been averted. Unbeknownst to them, the "disaster" was now deeply-rooted in my tender little heart. My parents' reaction had been to "forgive and forget." While I'm not certain about the "forgive" part, I do know that they wanted to minimize the situation and be done with it. I don't recall my parents ever speaking of the molestation again, other than during dinner conversation for the next couple of nights afterward. I think they were hoping that if they pretended to forget it, I would too.

THEY WERE HOPING THAT IF THEY PRETENDED TO FORGET IT, I WOULD TOO.

My siblings, however, had their own way of dealing what had happened to me. They were aware of the attempted rape and subsequent molestation and decided they were going to take matters into their own hands to ensure their little sister's safety. They invented a game that would give them an opportunity to act out just what they would do to our cousin should he ever dare threaten me again. Whenever my parents went out, they left my two older siblings in charge of me and my little brother. As soon as they were out the door, THE GAME would begin. We would arm ourselves with "weapons" such as small sticks, a cap gun or stuffed animals. We would find our hiding places, whether it be behind a door, under a table, or another vantage point to attack from. Pretending that my cousin had entered the house with malicious intent, we would suddenly spring from our hiding places and attack our imaginary foe, disabling him in all ways imaginable.

For my siblings, it was a fun-filled game, but for me it was something totally different. I watched as the situation that still imprisoned me became reduced to playful fantasy, a source of entertainment for them. My brothers and sister never meant to hurt me. It was their way of showing me that they would do all they could to protect me; however, that wasn't what it felt like. The shame and embarrassment cut deeply into my heart, carving out a place where I could hide and "feel safe" once again. It became my new normal. As time went on, I further separated myself from the pain, gaining so much distance from it that one day it seemed as if it had never happened at all! It became someone else's life; it was another little girl with curly blonde hair who had been violated. I had succeeded in convincing myself that the attacks no longer mattered and therefore could no longer affect me. Unfortunately, the truth was irrefutable. It had a definite impact and forever changed my life, whether I wanted to admit it or not.

A mentor once gave me wise counsel, "If you see the fruit, you have the root." There was plenty of "fruit" manifesting in my life. By nine years old, I was interested in pornography magazines and would allow older boys to touch me in ways that left me feeling defiled. By fifth grade, my boyfriend and I would routinely come up with reasons to slip off to my bedroom and close the door. Yes, of course we were acting inappropriately in there; yet amazingly, I somehow managed to remain a virgin. I didn't feel good about how I was acting, yet I felt powerless to change the path my life was taking. I frequently felt dirty and ashamed. To a trained observer, it would have been obvious that I was "broken." However, as the young and ignorant are wont to do, I vehemently denied that I was in any emotional pain.

Not only was I in emotional pain, I was in deep denial. I was being deceived. I felt that what had happened to that little girl was unfortunate, but it was history. It might have occurred, but it was a "forgotten" part of my past, no longer able to impact my present. Before starting college, I had already met the man I wanted to marry. Bob was two years older, and embodied everything I wanted in a husband. I was star-struck. We attended the same college and were married two years after my graduation.

SHAME LEADS TO ANGER

It was while we were living together in college, that anger—and occasionally rage—would rear its ugly head. During these episodes Bob would accuse me of being a totally different woman than the one he fell in love with. I felt as if I was seething, trapped inside a pressure-cooker with no release valve. As the relationship blossomed, with increasing sexual intimacy, I was required to let my walls down. As I lowered my guard, the internal pressure increased. It seemed as if I was angry all the time. I was a shaken soda bottle ready to explode. Bob really wasn't the source of my anger. I was angry at the world and he just happened to take the brunt of it whenever I spewed like a volcano. What I didn't realize at that time was that my unresolved issues, which I'd worked so hard to repress, were now starting to surface. I hated the way I was behaving, but seemed unable to control it.

It came to a head one night during my senior year of college. We were preparing dinner in our off-campus apartment. As usual, I was doing the cooking while Bob was cleaning up after me, washing the dishes. We started to argue over something so inconsequential I can't even recall what it was, when Bob suddenly declared, "ENOUGH IS ENOUGH!" He was sick and tired of my nasty attitude. Scooping up the soapy utensils, he hurled them at the wall. As they clattered to the floor, I watched a spoon's wooden handle break off upon impact. Our tableware was not rare or expensive by any stretch of the imagination; I had purchased it at a garage sale for a mere five dollars. However, when I saw that broken handle lying on the floor, something deep within me broke as well.

It did not make any rational sense, but Bob's actions left me feeling violated and dishonored. I felt he had deliberately broken something of great value, as I was trying so hard to make that apartment our home. I'd conveniently disregarded the fact that I had been pushing Bob to this point for a long time. A hot, fiery rage consumed me in that instant! In desperation, my eyes fell on the twelve-inch butcher knife I had been using to prepare dinner. Instantly, I knew what I wanted to do. I grabbed the handle and lunged at Bob. My intention was to bury that blade deep in his abdomen and pull it upward toward the sternum, effectively gutting him like a fish! Thankfully (trust me, I am still EXTREMELY grateful!), Bob recognized the murderous look in my eyes and knew I was dead serious. He dodged my crazed frontal attack with the agility of a gymnast. Just as quickly he pivoted and wrapped his arms around me from behind, prying the knife out of my clenched fist. I was furious! I screamed. I swore. I tried to break loose from his grasp, but I was no match for his strength. He held me tightly, giving me time to calm down. After a few minutes, I realized my struggling was futile and sanity slowly began seeping back into my mind. Bob waited until he was assured of my mental status, then gradually relaxed his grip. Although he had kicked the butcher knife safely out of my reach, it was no longer an issue. I had regained my senses and lost the desire to spill his blood.

It scares me to think of how differently things would have played out for us had Bob not been strong enough to overpower me. It had now become obvious to both of us that I was carrying huge, unresolved issues that needed to be confronted and addressed. However, in my obstinance, I retreated into my old familiar fortress of "ignore and disregard it." As a result, we just kept plowing forward, determined not to poke a sharp stick at the monster lurking within.

The issues in our sexual relationship were becoming increasingly difficult to ignore. The longer we were together, the more dysfunctional it became. From a sexual standpoint, I still felt dirty, used, embarrassed and ashamed. Fortunately, Bob had a healthy view of sexuality and kept trying to talk me through how unreasonable and irrational my feelings were. Just as I began to think I was making headway, he would initiate sex and I would drown in those feelings once again. I had always imagined that sexual intimacy with the only one I truly loved should automatically be free of any anxiety or problems. It was anything but that. As time passed, our moments of intimacy worsened, leaving me feeling panicky, trapped and violated. I was not yet at the point of being able to admit, much less understand, why I was feeling like that. That would come later, after I allowed God to repair my brokenness. Only then would I be empowered to understand my feelings and gain the objectivity necessary to uncover what was driving my unhappiness.

As our seventh anniversary neared, despite Bob's patience and desire to understand me, I knew that my behavior was destroying our marriage. We were sinking and we both knew it. I was getting desperate. I knew I had issues, but had no idea how to resolve them. At the same time, I was doing my best to stay in denial. How could a CHILDHOOD incident so strongly impact my ADULT life? I certainly didn't want to dwell on it or talk about it. I wanted to leave it where it was, in the past! A few years earlier, Bob and I had committed our lives to Christ. It had thrilled me to learn that we were now "new creatures," all of our sins and hurts "under the blood"—forgiven and forgotten! I had my own interpretation of that Scripture: now I had a valid excuse for not dealing with any of that ugliness in my past! Jesus had just guaranteed me a rosy future! In reality, neither of those were true.

I began to dread spending time alone with Bob. He was (and still is!) the love of my life, yet that seemed to make little difference to me. He still found me sexually desirable, but I avoided his advances like the plague. Whereas, in the past, we were quite comfortable being naked in each other's presence, I now found myself making excuses to hide my body and would undress under cover of darkness. Men are visually-driven and I knew that Bob seeing my naked body would take us down that slippery-slope I was so desperately trying to avoid. The chasm this was forming in our relationship was beginning to resemble the Grand Canyon. It was obvious to me that this was going to ruin my marriage if something didn't soon change.

One day out of desperation, I tuned to a Christian radio station and listened to Dr. Dobson's "Focus on the Family." On this particular day, a young woman was relating her story of being sexually molested as a little girl. She described the toll it had taken on her life and marriage because she hadn't ever dealt with it. I began to sense a personal connection on an emotional level, yet had no idea where this was leading. I had buried my own experience so deeply, I could hardly admit the reality of the attack to myself, much less to anyone else. I had done my best to block every memory of it. Years later, I would come to understand that "if you have the fruit, you have the root," but at that time, I had not equated the poor sexual dynamic of our marriage to my history of abuse.

> I HAD NOT YET EQUATED THE POOR SEXUAL DYNAMIC OF OUR MARRIAGE TO MY HISTORY OF ABUSE.

As I continued to listen to the woman recount her history, the Lord suddenly reminded me that I had experienced something similar. My first reaction was "NO WAY!" Still, I continued to listen. She related how God had led her to revisit the painful attack and then had proceeded to heal her of the deep wounding and heart issues. Once again, I yelled "NO WAY!" I was NEVER going back there ever! I felt like I had barely survived the first time; I was certainly in no hurry to relive it! Yet, I felt compelled to keep listening. By the end of the program, she praised her new-found freedom, the healing it had brought to her marriage and the gratitude she felt to the Lord. It was obvious by the emotion in her voice that she was being genuine and truthful.

KEY #1—FREEDOM IS A CHOICE

The program ended, but my thoughts of what I had just heard did not. I was terrified of my past, but I was more afraid for my future (and my marriage) if I did not confront it. I desperately wanted that freedom for myself! I sat crying next to the radio, not knowing how to proceed. Gently, I felt the Lord's presence come upon me. He was assuring me that if I dared to allow Him to take me back there, He would remain right by my side. Still, I was afraid. As I continued to sit in His presence, I slowly began to feel that I could trust Him with my pain. *Why not? I have nothing to lose. What I've been doing so far certainly hasn't been working.* My life felt like a train wreck and our marriage would soon become a divorce statistic. *Denial certainly isn't the answer, so why not confront it with the Lord's help?*

I closed my eyes and slowly let Him take me back to that time. To that room. To the first time I was violated. I could almost smell the fear. The guilt was thick and tangible. Suddenly, the presence of the Lord seemed to surround me and He spoke clearly to my heart, "It is NOT your fault!" I couldn't believe it! I just sat there in silence. Shockingly, the words began to pierce the very depths of my soul. Again I heard, "It is NOT your fault!" I had never allowed myself to acknowledge that I had been shouldering the blame all these years. No wonder physical intimacy left me feeling guilt-ridden, dirty and used. Again, God spoke His healing words to my heart, "It is not your fault," and this time … I believed them. The deeply-entrenched pain in my heart, which had been holding me captive for so many years, began to tear loose. I wept, my body wracked with deep, guttural sobs, and with each one I could feel shards of pain and guilt leaving. When I finally did stop crying, I felt a relief so immense it simply defied description. A peace I hadn't known since I was a little girl enveloped me. As I sat basking in the freedom only God can grant, He whispered His desire to restore the innocence and purity that had been stolen from me so long ago. I wept again, but this time with tears of joy. I felt Him wash me anew. I felt so clean! I felt … WHOLE!

That session with my Heavenly Father did more for our marriage than I could ever have imagined. Our sexual union became what God had always intended it to be. I no longer felt used. No panicky thoughts or feelings of violation sullied our lovemaking. I could finally receive and luxuriate in my husband's love! The first time we came together after my "healing," I started sobbing right in the middle of it because I could not believe the feeling of incredible love coursing through my being. I had no words for the freedom I was experiencing. Panic and dread were no longer part of our sexual relationship!

Because of all God walked me through to reclaim my freedom, I could now allow myself to fully trust Him. I could trust Him to make me whole in other areas of my life as well. I wasn't so naive as to think that I had attained perfection. I knew there were many other areas of my life that could use the Lord's healing touch. I decided then and there that I wanted to be the best person I could be. I wanted to reach my full potential and live a life of emotional well—being. I would forever trust God to heal my heart. I loved my new life of freedom and resolved that if He ever prompted me to deal with another wounding of my past, I would trust Him to take me through that experience as well.

The commitment I made that day has become a cornerstone in my life. He has proven to be the ever faithful, gentle Healer of my soul! That simple decision has produced an amazingly fruitful harvest in my life, more than I could ever have hoped for! He has never let me down or disappointed me.

His desire to see us walk in freedom transcends our limited understanding. A very wise man once offered me a bit of advice I will always treasure … "Heal your past; you'll redeem your future." I am living proof of that!

PRAYER FOR CHOOSING FREEDOM

Heavenly Father, you knew me even before I was born. You know everything about me. You know the good; You know the bad. Still You love me beyond imagination. Beyond what I can grasp. Father, You even know the events of my life that I consider the most shameful. The things I have tried my best to hide from others, and yes, even tried to hide from myself... Still, You love me.

Father, I no longer want to live as a broken individual. I see "fruit" in my life that I do not like. I may not even be fully aware of what the "root" is, but I know that You do. Today, Father, I CHOOSE to TRUST You. I CHOOSE to allow You to come to those places that I have so closely protected and guarded. Father, I CHOOSE to partner with You to become WHOLE.

Would You start, right now, to gently begin to expose those areas of brokenness to me? I invite You into those places of woundedness to do what You love to do best: bring HEALING! Father, I give You permission to take me back to those places of wounding. I give You permission to remove all hurt, all lies that I believed in my heart, all trauma, all brokenness. As You show me this, Father, I CHOOSE to release this heavy yoke I have been carrying. I realize it was never meant for me; Jesus Christ took this yoke upon himself at Calvary. So, Jesus, I give these burdens to you. I renounce the lies that the enemy of my soul planted in my heart. Father, in place of those lies I ask now for a heavenly exchange. What Truth would You like to share with me? What would You like to speak to my heart?

I release all shame, guilt, and any other feeling of defilement that the enemy cloaked me with. Father, I know You are the God of Exchange! What would You like to give me in exchange for these feelings? I CHOOSE to receive them! I CHOOSE to believe Your truth. I CHOOSE to receive Your forgiveness and love. As I sit here, Father, I ask that You would love upon me. Wrap me in Your arms.

I sever all association and power that those "Roots" and 'Fruits" wielded in my life. I receive the transforming power of Your love, and anxiously await the new harvest that will be rooted in Your love and wholeness.

I CHOOSE, Father, to let wholeness be a lifestyle for me. No longer will I hide from You and Your love. You are a good, good Father, and I can trust You. Amen.

TWO

LOVE IS MORE THAN AN EMOTION

CHOOSING TO ACT IN LOVE

"Love looks like something."

HEIDI BAKER

With the tremendous healing God had done in my heart regarding childhood molestation, you would think that our marriage would be repaired as well. Unfortunately, that was not the case. It would take almost seven years before that healing took place.

A tremendous amount of damage can occur to a relationship in seven years! We hurt each other deeply and eroded the foundation of love and trust that our relationship had been built on. If our marriage was going to be saved, it would take a God-sized miracle! Fortunately, that was exactly what God had in mind. The real question was, did we want it badly enough to do what we needed to do? It was during this season of our life that God taught me life-lesson number two: love is not simply an emotion, it is something I can CHOOSE and ACT ON.

During those years, I did many things to take the focus off of my own brokenness. I did and said many things to put the blame on Bob. Now, seven years later we were reaping the harvest of some very bad crops that we had sown earlier in our relationship. Some of those seeds had been intentional, some were sown out of ignorance. Regardless, we were dealing with serious issues of mistrust and alienation that we had never expected. Wisdom should have told me that my actions, motivated by brokenness and self-protection, would eventually destroy the love that we both deeply desired and needed.

I fabricated many "reasons" to explain why our sexual intimacy was not producing all the joy and love the world had promised us. Without exception, my justifications and excuses blamed Bob. Inwardly, I felt like a failure, too fragile and wounded to be blatantly honest, even with myself. Bob was my scapegoat; my distraction from the truth. I can still clearly recall some of the things I told Bob to try and convince him that he was the "problem." I accusingly proclaimed that he was the one lacking in the "intimacy" department. It was his fault that I did not enjoy sex. If we had allowed someone with more wisdom to see the inner workings of our relationship, they would have immediately seen through my smoke-screen.

OPENING A DOOR BEST LEFT CLOSED

I distinctly remember the summer day which proved to be the proverbial straw that broke the camel's back, putting us on a path of destruction that would take many years to restore. We were both in college and home for summer break. Bob was busy working on the restoration of a classic car, spending endless hours focusing on it instead of me. I was bored. I was lonely. As I had no vision or project like Bob did to occupy my time, I was also resentful. With all this free time on my hands, I decided I was going to "fix" this problem which produced such stress and so many arguments. I started reading Playboy magazines, thinking they just might hold the secret answer to our problem. Neither of us had a relationship with God at this point, so it made perfect sense to me.

Bob worked on his classic car, while I sat on the grass next to him and read one article after another. This continued until finally, one day it all erupted. I read an article describing how the problem with most women's poor response in the bedroom was due to the man not knowing how to meet her needs. I loved this article because it put all the blame right where I wanted it; on Bob! Adding insult to injury, I finished reading and proclaimed, "See Bob, it's just like I've been trying to tell you. The problem isn't me, it's you!"

Even while speaking, I knew it wasn't true, yet I was desperate to take the pressure off of myself. Bob stopped working on the car, looked up at me and asked, "So, you think I'm a lousy lover?" Back peddling, I replied, "No, not lousy. I just think if you were better in bed we wouldn't have all these problems." He didn't say a word. He didn't have to. I knew something terrible had just transpired between us. Something had been put into motion we would one day both regret.

A formidable chasm opened a great divide between us that day. I had unjustly attacked Bob at the very core of his manhood. It left him with two choices: either agree with my faulty accusation, or prove to himself that he was not lacking. He chose the latter option.

I had two girlfriends (I use that term loosely) that were both infatuated with Bob and had made it clear to him that they were "available." As the summer progressed, it became the perfect solution to him. He had no interest in a long-term relationship with either of them, but they could offer the answer to the question now tormenting him. Consequently, he ended up having sex with both of them. This settled two important issues for Bob. First, it assured him that my accusation had indeed been a lie. Secondly, it made him realize that as messed up as our relationship was, it was me that he loved and wanted to be with. He realized that infidelity was not for him. By nature, he was a "one-woman" man, and he wanted to live that lifestyle.

I had always believed that I was a "one-man" woman. I had never imagined that I could be unfaithful to my lover. Unfortunately, before all was said and done, I would discover that I did not know myself quite as well as I thought. Upon discovering Bob's unfaithfulness, I became furious! I felt betrayed. Had I been more insightful, I might have realized his betrayal was a natural response to what I had started ... Instead, I made two decisions. The first was to bury my devastation and do my best to go forward in our relationship. The second was that one day, Bob would know what this kind of painful devastation felt like. One day, I would take my revenge.

We graduated from college and found employment. A year later we were married. I think we both hoped that marriage would bridge the chasm that was ever-present in our relationship. We had become two very independent individuals. We did not trust, nor allow ourselves to be vulnerable with each other. We kept our finances separate. Our household bills were divided 50-50 to insure that no one was being taking advantage of. An added benefit was that there was no need to extend even financial trust to one another. In spite of this, we lived frugally and saved for a house.

It might seem strange to you that despite all the unrest between us, we were still planning a future together. As dysfunctional as we were, we knew beyond a shadow of a doubt that we belonged together and there was no one else in the world we would rather be with. We had met on a blind-date when he was 18 and I was one month shy of 17. We both knew within a half hour of meeting that we were going to spend the rest of our lives together. That sounds crazy, but it's true. We both sensed it, yet we never told each other until quite some time later. Still, despite all the animosity between us stemming from immaturity and bad choices, we always had a tenacious commitment. That may have been the only thing that kept our relationship from totally imploding.

Two years after our wedding, we purchased an old farmhouse that needed major restoration. Bob jumped into it feet-first. He woke up before dawn, started working on it, then left for his job, only to return home and work on the house once again until after midnight. This was his normal routine. He was determined to do it himself, and was determined to get it done. However, this left no time for us. If I wanted to see him, I had to be wherever he was working or work along-side him, which was fine. Well, it was fine for the first year or so, but eventually it got old. He was stressed trying to get such a big project done (it ended up taking him seven years), and I was stressed because there seemed to be no relationship between the two of us. Eventually my emotional love tank hit empty and I started looking elsewhere for attention.

I was a bitter and lonely young woman. I had never forgiven Bob for being unfaithful to me, and still desired revenge. Slowly, a plan began to form in my mind ... Bob and I had a male friend we were both very close to and spent a lot of time with. He was kind, thoughtful and single. He seemed like the perfect solution. I would kill two birds with one stone. I would not feel so lonely and love-starved, and Bob would learn the pain of betrayal (How could I have been so blind?).

INSTEAD OF FEELING LOVED AND HAPPY, I CONSTANTLY FELT GUILTY.

I executed my plan, but it certainly was not the solution! It complicated everything. Bob and I had just recently committed our lives to Christ Jesus, and had started regularly attending church and Bible study. The fact that I was committing adultery bumped up against my new-found faith and created a huge dichotomy within. Instead of feeling loved and happy, I constantly felt guilty. Despite the fact that I deeply cared about this man, I could not ignore that this affair was in complete opposition not just to my faith, but also to his best interest! I felt badly for what I was doing to this man, what I was doing to my relationship with God, and what I was doing to my husband. Not being able to live with the hypocrisy any longer, I ended the affair. With fear and trembling, I told Bob what I had done. His response was the complete opposite of what I had expected. He looked me in the eyes and told me he forgave me, that he loved me, and he wanted to work things out.

GUILT IS A PRISON

You might think Bob let me off too easily, but I can assure you there was nothing easy about it! I had braced for his rage. I had even braced for a tirade of hate-filled accusations and comments. I had emotionally prepared myself, for I felt I deserved it. When he responded with nothing but love, kindness and forgiveness, it was more than I could bear. Despite the amazing forgiveness and grace Bob was offering me, I could not accept it. I KNEW I didn't deserve it. Inwardly, I felt that I deserved some kind of punishment, not being forgiven and let off the hook. I obviously had no understanding of God's grace and forgiveness. To have the very person I had deliberately hurt offer me his forgiveness emotionally devastated me. Instead of feeling happy and free, I had a nagging sense of unworthiness following me. I deserved to be punished, yet I wasn't. It didn't seem right, and I wouldn't allow myself to accept the gift that Bob so freely offered.

As a result, although Bob made efforts to try and bring healing to our marriage, I was unable to fully engage. The more he tried to love me, the guiltier I felt. I could not connect on a deep emotional level. I was still lonely (so was Bob) and I started missing my relationship with the other man. Before long I rekindled the affair. I don't know why I thought I would feel any better about it the second time around, but of course, if my reasoning had been solid, I wouldn't have found myself there in the first place ... Although I deeply cared for this man, I once again felt unbearable guilt and knew what I was doing was terribly wrong. I ended it once again, feeling awful about the pain and destruction my actions were causing both men.

All I had really managed to do was complicate an already complicated bad situation, and further wound our marriage. I knew, beyond a shadow of a doubt, that I was an emotional mess and needed to find serious help. I met with our pastor, Jerry, and told him what I had done. He knew about my initial affair and was saddened to learn that I had resumed it. I confided that I was afraid to tell Bob. He had been so forgiving the first time and I didn't think he would offer the same response again. Our marriage was holding on by a thread and I really didn't think it could survive this. Pastor Jerry agreed that I should consider waiting a bit before I confessed the news to Bob. He thought I should give our relationship a chance to get on firmer ground before I dropped the bomb. I agreed, very relieved that I did not immediately need to have that conversation. My pastor agreed to start meeting with me once a week, to sort out some of my issues. I was grateful that there was someone willing to not just help me, but who also believed there was hope for our marriage.

I was now ready to start looking deep within and to do whatever I needed to change. I wanted our marriage to work, but had no idea how to make that happen. God seemed to be the only viable answer left. Since I had tried everything else, I decided to give God a chance. Although I had accepted Christ a year or so earlier, I had not taken God all that seriously. I had a very shallow view of Christ's sacrifice and what being a disciple entailed. My theology was simple: I said a prayer, was forgiven and earned my ticket to heaven. I figured that sinning was no big deal, as all I had to do was recite another quick prayer, ask to be forgiven, and everything would once again be great. However, now that I was personally experiencing the ramifications of my deceptive actions and poor decisions, I was starting to re-think my entire belief system. If my previous doctrine was correct and this was true Christianity, then I knew it was a farce. If it was not true Christianity, then something, or more precisely, someone needed to change.

Before Pastor Jerry and I had started meeting, two things occurred along my journey that would change both the course of my life and the future of my marriage. The first was when I opened my Bible to Jeremiah 29:13-14 and read, *"And you will seek Me and find Me, when you search for Me with all your heart. I will be found by you, says the LORD, and I will bring you back from your captivity."* I had never truly sought after God with ALL my heart, and honestly, I had no idea how to start! I certainly felt like I was a prisoner of my foolish decisions. I NEEDED to be rescued from the captivity I had created! Determined to hang onto the thread of life that still existed in our marriage, I took the Scripture seriously. Secondly, I decided to do a self-guided Bible study, by a well-known author. The study entailed discovering the attributes of a "Woman of Excellence," using Proverbs 31 as the basis. I figured I was about as far from being a woman of excellence as you could ever imagine, but maybe I could learn something that would help me change.

Pastor Jerry and I started meeting weekly, and I took it seriously. I listened to what he told me, took to heart the advice and wisdom he shared, and did any homework he suggested. He would challenge me, encourage me, and sometimes tell me things that I didn't appreciate, but knew to be true. I was fully engaged; I wanted to grow, I wanted to change! My homework would often include reading and memorizing Scripture, reflecting on areas of my life, or doing something very practical to stabilize our marriage. It was around this time that God healed me from the trauma of childhood molestation. I was definitely making some positive progress and so was our marriage, but I knew the healing would be limited without complete truth and transparency between Bob and myself. I absolutely dreaded the day I was going to have to tell him about my relapse, but at the same time I knew it was essential.

Finally, the day came. With fear and trepidation I told him what I had done. He didn't say a word. He didn't tell me he loved me like he did the first time either. He didn't say he forgave me. He sat there, wordlessly. Finally, he got up and walked away. I knew we were in deep trouble. He told me many years later that he went to bed that night but could not sleep. All night long he laid there, planning how he would leave me, get a divorce, and start a new life with a woman that would not only love him, but be faithful to him. He didn't sleep a wink. Finally, just as dawn was breaking he said God clearly spoke to him and said, "You are not going anywhere. The problem in your marriage is at least 50% your fault as well. You're not going anywhere. You are going to stay and work this out." It scares me to think of what would have unfolded if Bob had not had that God-encounter.

REVENGE LEADS TO REGRET

When I woke up the next morning, Bob was still not speaking to me. I was walking on eggshells. You could cut the tension with a knife. I had no idea about what had transpired the previous night. All I knew was that he did not mention divorce, which really surprised me. Still, things were far from good. Bob now fully understood the pain of having an unfaithful partner. I had taken my revenge, accomplished my goal, and now deeply regretted it. Regret did not take away the pain or the devastation. Any fragile piece of intimacy we had previously gained was now completely shattered. Although God had told Bob he was not to leave physically, he left me emotionally. The loneliness I had felt before the affair was nothing compared to the loneliness I now felt. I had no one. Not my former lover. Not my husband. Not my friend.

There was one relationship that I was determined NOT to lose, and that was my relationship with God. If I was going to learn to be faithful and trustworthy, I knew it had to start there. I continued to meet with Pastor Jerry, do Bible study on my own, and read the Bible in earnest. I was not seeing any visible signs of improvement between Bob and me, yet I was determined I was not going to quit. Actually, things seemed much worse between the two of us. The apathy had now turned to hostility, even hatred. Bob didn't even want to be in the same room with me, and never looked into my eyes. The love that we had once shared seemed so distant that I could not even remember what it felt like. We simply co-existed as unhappy roommates. We spoke only if there was a need to share information. Weeks turned into months. It was now over a year since I had told him about the affair, and the situation seemed hopeless.

> I DIDN'T SEE HOW GOD COULD BRING ANY GOOD OUT OF THE TERRIBLE MESS I HAD MADE.

Right around this time, I shockingly had a God-encounter of my own! I went to bed one night reading the Psalms. I could relate to David's hopelessness. Tears started rolling down my cheeks and utter despair filled my heart. I had always felt confident in my ability to eventually escape any problems that came my way. Admittedly, I was not as wise as I thought I was, but this time I was without a solution. Everything I tried dug a deeper hole. There was nothing I could do to manipulate, control, or connive my way out of this mess. I put down the Bible, buried my head in my pillow so Bob would not hear me cry, and told God I was done. If I was going to have to live the rest of my life in this state, I wanted my life to end. I didn't see any other option. I didn't see how God could bring any good out of the terrible mess I had made. Actually, I wasn't even sure He was willing to.

You see, it wasn't just that I was unable to receive grace and forgiveness from Bob, but I couldn't receive it from God either. In my heart, I thought He was done with me; that He was disgusted and fed-up. I knew I didn't deserve Jesus' sacrifice on the cross, nor His love. I knew I had trampled them both underfoot and didn't think he was a God of "second chances." I fell asleep on my tear-stained pillow. At 3:05 AM I suddenly awoke. I had just had a powerful dream and I without a doubt KNEW it was from God! I have no idea how I knew that, I just did. In the dream, God took me back to my decision to first commit adultery. He showed me the devastation it caused, and then the even greater devastation I caused by going back to this man. The enemy of my soul was dressed in black clothes with a black hoodie pulled low over his face during the entire dream. Every time I would try and free myself from his grasp or influence he would inevitably outwit me and cause my body to weaken by degrees. By the end of the dream, he left me for dead alongside the road, jumped into an old car, and made his escape. All that kept going through my mind was that I needed to stay alive long enough to be able to tell the people I loved what had happened to me. I also needed to be able to convey his identity to them so they would know who had been responsible. With this in mind, weakly I lifted up my head and saw his license plate lit by the taillights as he sped away. I started repeating the license plate over and over in my mind so I would not forget it. Over and over I repeated it, and that is how I woke up.

I looked at that clock—3:05 AM. I dropped my head back on the pillow, still in a daze and said, "God, what did that mean? Would You interpret that?" Instantly, He took me back to the beginning of the dream and started narrating. My guess is the interpretation took only a minute at the most, but it seemed much longer than that. He told me several things that would change my life forever, but that is a story for a different time. What I want to share with you right now is the importance of the license plate that I kept repeating. The license plate was "ADJ AE 7/6" and God told me the "ADJ" meant adjustment and that He was going to make an adjustment in my thought-life. He then brought my attention to the "AE." He reminded me that all my life it had been very important to me to try to be perfect. Starting in kindergarten and continuing throughout my college years, it was vital to me to achieve perfect grades on my papers. I remember being a little girl, running home from school each Friday with the fistful of papers I had completed that week. I would climb onto my daddy's lap and proudly display them all.

We would go through them one by one, and he would show exaggerated excitement over each paper that was graded with an "E." (When I was young the grading system was E for excellence, S for satisfactory, and U for unsatisfactory.). As far as I was concerned, only "E" papers mattered, as my dad would give me a nickel for each one! I received nothing for an "S" paper, so I strove for perfection. My father never meant to create a spirit of striving within me, it was just a fun game we played together every Friday evening. They were filled with lots of laughs, "OHH's and AWW's." I loved it. Yet, the need to be perfect continued throughout high school, into college years and permeated my professional career.

Now, here I was, an adult, and I had really messed things up. God brought my attention back to the license plate: ADJ AE 7/6. He highlighted the number 7 that stood directly over the number 6 (like a fraction). He told me to look at it. When I did, a cascading shower of red began to flow from the number 7 onto the 6, covering it in the most beautiful way. I instantly understood that the number 7 represented Jesus and the number 6 represented mankind. He then spoke to me and said that because I had chosen to accept Jesus as my Lord and Savior, I had placed myself under the protective umbrella of His blood. He told me to look at it again and now all I could see was the number 7 and the beautiful scarlet waterfall of mercy cascading downward. I could not see the 6 at all, yet knew it was there. He then explained that because I was under the blood of Jesus, God saw me as an "A" and an "E." He saw me as perfect! I was accepted, I was loved!

SWEET REPENTANCE

Comforted by a deep sense of peace, I immediately fell back to sleep. I woke up the next morning and knew my life would never be the same. I no longer had to fear that God was going to cast me aside and send me to hell for my foolishness. I had repented, I had chosen to leave that lifestyle, and I now KNEW I was loved and forgiven. Romans 2:4 says,

"Do the riches of his extraordinary kindness make you take him for granted and despise him? Haven't you experienced how kind and understanding he has been to you? Don't mistake his tolerance for acceptance. Do you realize that all the wealth of his extravagant kindness is meant to melt your heart and lead you into repentance?" (TPT).

It was clear to me now that the foolish theology I had previously embraced, thinking grace was cheap and that I could live anyway I wished, was just that: foolishness! Repentance was sweet to me. The thought of leaving the hopelessness of my old ways opened up new possibilities that had previously seemed impossible. Whereas the night before I had gone to bed wanting to end my life, I now dared to believe that someday I might even have a bright future! I wanted to live, and God was beginning to position me for hope. To date, nothing had changed between Bob and me, but as God had predicted, I had received a HUGE spiritual adjustment, and was now positioned to do what He would require of me.

One week, during my session with Pastor Jerry, he gave me an unusual homework assignment. Although I was now starting to believe that God loved and accepted me, Jerry sensed my inability to transfer that love to Bob in a tangible way. He instructed me to consult my Strong's Concordance, looking up every verse in the Bible containing the word love, and write each one out. I was aghast! He encouraged me not to tackle this assignment like something I had to conquer and finish quickly, but rather, take my time and meditate on what I discovered. "It may take several weeks, but that is okay", he said. I got out a notebook and started to write the reference and then the verse. If a certain Scripture spoke to my heart, I would jot down what came to mind. He was right. This was going to take weeks! I was OVERWHELMED by the number of verses in the Bible having the word love in them! Still, I had decided I was going to seek God with all my heart, and was I serious about this, so I persevered.

Amazingly, as I worked my way through the Old Testament verses, and began in the New Testament, God started challenging my definition of love. I had always believed that love was an emotion; a feeling that made you giddy and happy inside when you thought of that special someone. The feeling of being on top of the world. Well, I certainly didn't feel any of those things toward Bob, and it was obviously mutual! When I got to the Book of John, my previous definition of love really started to unravel. In John 14:15 it says, *"If you love Me, keep My commandments,"* and it totally rocked my world! Suddenly, it seemed love had less to do with how a person felt, and more to do with what the person did. I couldn't believe it. It was the opposite of what I had always believed! Here, in this Scripture, God was saying that if you loved Him you did something—you kept His commandments. Love was an action, not a feeling like I had always believed! The evidence of the love was action, not the warm and fuzzy chick-flick feeling I'd always imagined. God again spoke to my heart saying that if I took action, the feelings would eventually follow, but they were not to be my barometer. This was a huge paradigm shift for me!

I was so excited and I couldn't stop thinking of what God had revealed to me about love. I called Pastor Jerry and left a long message on his answering machine telling him of my new discovery. I'm sure I sounded a bit crazy, but I couldn't contain my excitement. I told Bob too, but he was not impressed, as he had seen very few acts of love from me in the past few years. I didn't know what to do with this new-found information, but I knew it was pivotal.

A few days later, I was in our family room working on my "Woman of Excellence" Bible study when I came across a reference to Proverbs 12:4. The verse says, *"An excellent wife is the crown of her husband, but she who causes shame is like rottenness to his bones."* My heart sank. I knew all about causing Bob shame, and knew from experience that the latter portion of this verse was absolutely true. The first part though ...

did I even dare to dream? Was it even possible that one day I could be considered a "crown" to him? An excellent wife? That goal seemed too lofty for me, yet something in my heart yearned for it. I prayed a desperate prayer to God, that if at all possible, could He do a miracle causing me to somehow become an excellent wife? It seemed like an awful lot to ask, yet I figured that miracles were possible. The next day, the study-guide started teaching about Proverbs 31:10-12, *"Who can find a virtuous wife? For her worth is far above rubies. The heart of her husband safely trusts her, so he will have no lack of gain. She does him good and not evil all the days of her life."* Ugh ... this again tore my heart into pieces, as I knew I was about as far from a virtuous wife as one could get. Yet once again I thought, if anyone could change me, God could.

I sat there on the couch and cried out to God. Tears freely fell from my cheeks. I felt like such a failure as a wife, yet wanted to be so much more to Bob. As impossible as it seemed, I asked God to help me be the type of wife I had just read about. I asked Him to help Bob feel love for me again. That last request was answered in a way I certainly didn't expect. Immediately, a thought came to my heart: LOVE HIM! I thought, NO WAY! He doesn't even LIKE me anymore! He will reject me AND my love, God!

LOVE LIKE JESUS

Suddenly, a warm blanket of love enveloped me. Warm tears streamed down my cheeks. I hadn't felt this gentle kind of love in a long, long time, if ever. I simply sat there unmoving, basking in the feeling. Then, I felt Him speak to my heart and say, "You just be obedient and love Bob. Even if he rejects you and never loves you back it will be okay, because I love you and will be the Lover of Your Soul." Wow—I was floored! I could hardly believe what I had experienced, what I had just heard. Despite my hesitancy to do what He had just asked, I was certain that the love I had experienced was real, and that I could trust my Heavenly Father. It WAS going to be okay. The deep void of emotional hunger and loneliness I had felt for so many years was now filled in a way I had never imagined. If there had been a lingering feeling in my heart of being unloved or unaccepted, it was now completely gone! This experience, combined with the dream God had given me, solidified my belief deep within my heart. Possibly for the first time in my life I felt secure and KNEW I was deeply loved. Suddenly, the thought of Bob rejecting my attempts to love him no longer terrified me. I knew that I could risk loving Bob, and even if he rejected me I would not be devastated.

I closed the study book and decided there was no time like the present to start my assignment from the Lord. I went downstairs. Bob was sitting at the dining room table. Our marriage was so damaged by this point that when one of us entered the space of the other, the tension became palpable. You could actually feel the hostility and near-hatred. This time was no different. Bob was sitting there reading. You could visibly tell that his peace had been disturbed. My heart started to thump within my chest, yet I remembered God's promise that He would love me no matter what.

I quietly walked behind Bob's chair, and stood there trying to gather my courage. He of course ignored me, because that is what we did to each other. It was the strangest thing; I stood there behind Bob, not knowing how to show him love. What had once been so familiar between us was now completely foreign. The thought of touching him seemed so wrong, yet I knew I needed to obey God. Taking a deep breath, I walked the last few feet and stood directly behind him. Mustering all my strength and willpower, I carefully put my arms around him and gave him a cautious hug from behind. It was like hugging a bronze statue. He didn't move a muscle; he didn't blink an eye. He just kept right on reading as though I wasn't even there. I held the hug for less than 30 seconds, then let go and walked into the kitchen.

I had been right; Bob rejected me. The surprising part, however, was that I was OKAY! I knew in my heart that regardless, God was the lover of my soul! Just as He had promised, He seemed to once again envelop me in His love and comfort me. I might have been rejected by Bob, but this time I did not internalize the rejection. Bob might not ever return my love, but I knew right then and there that I would continue to be obedient and demonstrate love through my actions. The next day, Bob was standing in the kitchen, and I once again walked up behind him and gave him a hug. Once again, he rejected me. Not only did he stand motionless, this time he actually STIFFENED under my touch. He didn't want any part of me touching him, his body language shouted it loud and clear. Despite that, I was shocked to realize that once again it was well with my soul.

This continued for two full weeks! I would hug him several times each day, or offer some sort of meaningful touch, and each time it would be met with the wordless stiffening of his body. Yet each time, God would remind me that He was the lover of my soul, that He would love me even if Bob rejected me for the rest of my life. Finally, one day when I gave Bob a hug, I could feel his body soften just a bit. I was elated, and could barely believe what I had felt. A few days later, he touched my arm with his hand when I hugged him! It wasn't long after, he started to return my hugs, feebly at first. Despite how limp his arms were, they had never felt so good to me! I was incredibly grateful that I had been faithfully obedient.

What surprised me the most was that my feelings of love toward Bob were starting to return. I hadn't felt that for so long it actually caught me off guard! I had been so focused on the fact that love is an action and not a feeling that I had been prepared to walk out our relationship simply showing Bob I loved him. I had gone from one extreme to the other, but God was about to show me how to walk down the center of the road. For several years I was frustrated because I did not feel any love for Bob, yet once I started doing things God's way, the feeling started to grow like spring grass! It seemed too easy; too good to be true! And even more surprisingly, it was obvious that Bob was beginning to feel the same way toward me.

It has been nearly 30 years since I learned that love is an action. Without a doubt, it rescued our marriage. It taught me to choose to act in love, especially when I don't want to. I'm not perfect at this, but to the best of my ability I have chosen it as a way of life. Every relationship has it difficulties, whether it is a marriage or a friendship. Choosing to walk in love has resulted in consistency and stability even when faced with a challenging season. I have learned not to only follow my emotions, as I then become easily offended. Instead, I do what I know to be right and show the person love, even when it is the opposite of what I feel like doing.

KEY #2—LOVE IS A CHOICE

Over and over God has amazed me with the way He has honored my choices. Relationships have not only been rescued, they have flourished! My life used to be riddled with broken and unhealthy relationships. All relationships-marriage, friendship, and family-experience seasons of emotional ebb and flow. This used to rock my world, leaving me very insecure in the relationship. Consequently, my feelings toward the person would also begin to change. This would make me feel like I had failed in the relationship, and subsequently I would withdraw from it. Before long, the other person would become offended or feel rejected, and the relationship would begin to sink. This scenario was so predictable that I dreaded forming new friendships, as I knew it would eventually result in another person being angry with or disappointed in me. It was a terrible cycle to be stuck in. I could see the cycle, knowing that I was the common denominator, yet I had no idea how to change or break it.

Once God taught me to act in love regardless of whether or not the relationship was experiencing turbulence, that cycle in my life was completely broken. I no longer get rattled if the landscape of the relationship changes for a season. I don't get nervous and/or feel rejected. My identity is now secure in the love of the Father. The thought of rejection no longer holds me hostage. Therefore, I am able to continue to show the person love, acceptance and genuine kindness. The sensation of my life as an emotional roller-coaster is gone, and I can assure you that I don't miss it! I sometimes regret that I didn't learn this key to freedom earlier in my life, yet the fruit of walking in this has been incredible and nothing short of miraculous.

Ephesians 3:20-21 says, *"Now to him who is able to do exceedingly abundantly above all that we ask or think, according to the power that is at work in us, to Him be glory in the church by Christ Jesus to all generations, forever and ever. Amen."* God has certainly done more than I could ever have imagined as He has changed the way I love people. I have found that love in action is a reflection of God's heart, and the rewards are great. I never require people to love me in return. Of course I appreciate when they reciprocate, but I don't need it, as God is the lover of my soul. This frees people from my expectations or feeling obligated to act in a particular manner. However, the funniest thing usually happens ... I have noticed that when I love people with my actions, not expecting anything in return, people naturally want to reciprocate. This results in being surrounded with loving friendships and relationships filled with more blessings than I could have ever anticipated!

PRAYER FOR CHOOSING TO LOVE

Heavenly Father, it is your desire to be the Lover of our souls and to teach us what true love is. I confess that I have often chosen not to act in love. I repent of that and ask Your forgiveness. Father, I am not even sure that I truly understand love as you see it... I choose to open my heart to Your presence. Would you teach me to love like You do? With no agenda and no strings attached.

Father, it is impossible to love others if we do not first know that You love us. So, I choose to open up my heart to Your love. Would You show me how much You love me? Surround me and envelop me with Your love and presence. Speak to my heart and tell me of Your love. Still my heart, Father, as I allow You to minister to me. Touch me deep in my heart, where no man can touch. Thank you Daddy.

Father, there are areas in my heart where I have felt rejected and unloved. Would You increase Your presence right now and heal those areas of my heart? I ask You to re-nurture me in those areas and do an exchange that only You can do. Would you remove those areas of hurt and exchange them with Your love and presence? Thank you Daddy.

Now, Father, I ask that you would use me as an instrument of love and healing to others. Out of the abundance of love that You have poured into my heart, I ask that it would overflow to all those around me. Let my actions of love change the lives of others. I bring all my current and future relationships before Your Throne and ask You to bless and prosper them as I choose to be a living instrument of love in Your hands.

Your Word says that You do exceedingly and abundantly more than we can ever expect or imagine, so Father, I am asking that You do that for me and my relationships. Change me, and use me to change the world around me! Amen.

LOVE REGARDLESS,
WITH NO EXPECTATIONS
OF RECIPROCATION,
AND WATCH WHAT
GOD WILL DO!

THREE

REMOVING THE MASK
CHOOSING TRANSPARENCY AND VULNERABILITY

"The result of deceiving others is to live in fear of them."
MIKE MASON

"Let the inner movement of your heart always be to love one another, and never play the role of an actor wearing a mask."
ROMANS 12:9, TPT

I began to learn the importance of transparency and vulnerability as Bob and I were beginning to make progress in the healing of our marriage. Looking back, I now realize that the healing would have been very limited had I not chosen to embrace this new lifestyle.

The lesson of transparency came first. Webster defines being transparent as, "able to be seen through, easy to notice or understand, honest and open; not secretive." At that point in my life, the words transparent and Cinda did not belong in the same sentence. It was very important to me to be accepted and well-liked. As a result, I would often do or say what I thought others expected of me or what I thought might please them. I was insecure, yet did everything I could to hide that weakness. I wanted people to think I was kind, patient, smart, loving, interesting, funny. In other words, I wanted people to think I was perfect. I spent so much time managing my image that I only managed to confuse myself! I couldn't be honest with anyone else because I couldn't be honest with myself. I allowed people to know the image I projected, not my authentic self.

The only person who truly knew me intimately was my husband. He and our three young daughters lived with my "Jekyll and Hyde" persona 24/7. In public, I would be caring and loving. While at home I was impatient, angry, short-tempered and tyrannical. It wasn't a pretty sight! For whatever reason, Bob chose not to expose me for the hypocrite I was. My girls were too young to fully comprehend-much less verbalize-what they were experiencing. I thought I had everything under control, or should I say, under my manipulation? Little did I know that my carefully-constructed world was about to implode.

At this point, Bob and I had been married for nearly fifteen years. We had committed ourselves to Christ ten years earlier and were very active in our church of two hundred members. Church involvement was very important to me, because it fed my insecure and fragile ego. Simply put, I needed to be needed. I needed to be important. I needed to be well-liked … I needed so many things. We were committed to this church, operating in leadership positions.

Bob and I handled these leadership positions very differently. Bob was quite secure in who he was and always had been. He said what he meant and meant what he said. He didn't let people's opinions of him influence his integrity or decisions. I envied (and secretly hated) that about him! There was never any pretense with Bob; what you saw was what you got. He was honest through and through, sometimes even to a fault. People's opinions mattered to him, but he would never compromise his integrity to please them. How he ever put up with me, I will never know, but you can only imagine the tension it caused in our relationship.

To his credit, while in public, Bob never exposed my lack of integrity. I think he realized that sooner or later I would end up exposing it myself. In the meantime, all was not well on the home-front. We would usually fight on our drive to and from church. While in church, I would act the role of the perfect wife and mother. My acting had an emotionally-downward pull on Bob as he was disgusted and angered by my hypocrisy. People would sense his irritation with me, but have no idea as to the reason. Therefore they believed his irritation to be unfounded and considered him to be a jerk. Nothing could have been further from the truth, but I was pleased with the conclusions they were forming.

One day I felt like I had reached the pinnacle of my charade. We were at church and I was acting as usual (irritating Bob). An older woman came up to me as I was leaving and said, "Oh, Cinda, I thought being married to Jack was bad, but he is nothing compared to Bob! I feel so badly for you!" I can't begin to tell you how affirmed that comment made me feel. I felt like I had finally accomplished my goal: to convince everyone what a wonderful, perfect person I was. Bob had no idea about the comment she had made. All the way home I replayed the scenario over and over in my mind, and it felt so good. Little did I know that within a month everyone would begin to see the real me, and my facade would be exposed for what it really was.

NOWHERE TO HIDE

Bob and I had become friends with a couple, our age, at church. We spent a lot of time in their company. Her birthday was approaching and I wanted to do something special. Consulting my calendar, I noticed that her birthday happened to fall on the same day they attended Bible Study at our Pastor's house. Initially I was disappointed, but then a plan began to formulate in my mind ... if I hosted a surprise birthday party for her afterward, I could kill two birds with one stone. It would make my friend happy, in addition to proving to everyone in attendance what an amazing and caring person I was! This was important to me because most of the attendees were in leadership roles at the church. I looked up to them and wanted them to admire me as well. Bob was not onboard with my plan. He preferred we do something privately with the couple, but I would not concede. So, the arrangements were made, and off we went!

The group had been studying Stu Webber's "Tender Warrior" audio and workbook. On that night they were listening to a tape in which Webber was primarily addressing the men. He maintained that they were not living up to who God called them to be, and if there were any problems either at church or at home, he placed the blame squarely on the men's shoulders! I loved this point of view, as it reinforced the lie I had been living at church. I wanted everyone to think Bob was the problem and I loved that Stu Webber was agreeing with me! However, as the night progressed, I could sense the growing tension between us, and I realized I had better keep my opinions to myself.

I felt a storm brewing, and I certainly did not want it to erupt in front of forty people! All was well until a young woman started to voice her disappointment in men and her low opinion of them. Bob started to disagree with her accusations, and before you knew it, the two of them were involved in a heated debate. I was holding my breath, as I knew this topic was dangerous ground. Relief washed over me as I saw Bob decide to back down from the argument, keeping his opinions to himself. Just as things calmed down, the birthday girl's husband rekindled the discussion and the tension once again escalated. Bob was quiet, although I knew he had plenty to say. Her husband then turned to Bob and asked, "What do you think about this whole topic?" *OH NO!* It was too late. Bob replied, "I'll tell you what I think! The women are being led to believe that the problems in both the church and home are the men's fault. They are talking out of both sides of their mouths!! They act one way in church, but on the way back home, they become totally different women! If they walked in honesty and integrity in their own lives, I believe these problems would take care of themselves!"

I thought I was going to die! He never mentioned my name; he didn't have to. All eyes focused on me. They knew he wasn't just talking about women in general, he was specifically referring to the one he knew best! I felt naked and exposed. Everyone I craved approval from now had a front-row view to my apocryphal play. If there had been a hole large enough, I would have crawled into it!

The mood of the party had suddenly shifted and an uncomfortable silence now filled the room. What more was there to say? Everyone could sense the air was emotionally-charged. They knew that a major marital fight loomed on the horizon. In desperation, someone tried telling jokes to lighten things up. Thankful for the distraction, another person suggested we have some birthday cake and ice cream. I was devastated, my only objective being to survive the evening with my pride (yes, unfortunately, my pride) intact.

I could have been nominated for an Oscar that night. Instead of sobbing uncontrollably, which is what I desperately wanted to do, I plastered a fake smile on my face. I was acting my best to convince them that Bob's words were in no way directed at me or my lack of integrity. Looking back, I now realize that I didn't fool anyone; only myself. I held it together until most had left, when a very dear friend hugged me, and simply said, "I'm sorry." That was all I needed to become unglued! The floodgate of tears burst wide open. I sobbed on her shoulder. To hear my friend tell me that she was sorry, validated my feelings. I was still right and Bob was still wrong.

The atmosphere in our car was emotionally cold and dead quiet. I cried. Bob said nothing. When I did quit crying long enough to accuse Bob of this latest injustice, he simply stated that he had told the truth. We were at an impasse, both too stubborn to concede any ground.

Nothing changed during the next two days. Without exaggeration, I cried almost every waking moment. I was so incredibly embarrassed that I just wanted to disappear off the face of the earth. I NEVER wanted to go back to that church ever again, and I certainly never wanted to face anyone who had witnessed that night! Feeling sorry for myself, I was totally convinced that I was the victim. I tried explaining my position to Bob and how devastated his words had made me feel. I tried using word-pictures to convey my feelings, but nothing convinced Bob. He just didn't seem to understand my pain. I continued to start my mornings by crying all over again. I was grateful Bob had to work, leaving me alone with my tears. Halfway through the third day, teary-eyed as usual, God suddenly and unexpectedly spoke to my heart, "You know, you wouldn't be feeling so devastated about this whole thing if you had just been honest with people. Bob didn't say anything that wasn't true. All he did was expose how you've been living. If you had chosen to walk in transparency there would have been nothing left to expose."

I was shocked! I could not believe what I had just heard, so in His kindness, God repeated Himself ... Wow, this changed everything! I had never even considered this! What a paradigm shift! I then realized that I was not a victim, but had CHOSEN to give others the power to expose me as I had been living a lie. Truly, I was amazed by the light bulb He had just illuminated. This changed everything! Suddenly, I no longer was victimized, I felt empowered!

KEY #3—TRANSPARENCY IS A CHOICE

I made a life-changing decision right then and there. I would never again allow another person to wield power over my life! I would never again live behind a mask, pretending to be anyone other than myself. From now on I would live a life of transparency; a life of truth. By this, I would set myself free! If people liked me for who I was, great. If they didn't, at the end of the day I would still like myself.

Bob came home that night to a different wife. Whereas I had been crying and having a pity-party, I now possessed a new vision and purpose for my life. Bob came through the door and I couldn't wait to tell him what happened. I told him of my decision to live authentically, thereby denying others the power to expose me. He listened as I talked. I told him I forgave him for the seemingly cruel way he had exposed me to all the leadership. I told him I was even thankful it had happened, for I knew that from now on, my life was going to be different. I told him that as much as I wanted people's approval, it was more important that I liked and approved of myself. Although this was the way Bob had always lived, he had the good sense not to say, "I told you so!"

Walking in truth and transparency had always been a hallmark of Bob's character, and it excited me to know that I too, would someday be known for living with integrity as well. Was it scary at first? You bet. But each and every time I felt scared, I remembered what it felt like to constantly live in fear of someone exposing the "real me." I remembered how much energy it took to wear that mask of deception, and it hardened my resolve to never act that role again. I realized the new vision of my future far outweighed any fear I may experience. Eventually, transparency became a habit. I stayed true to myself and therefore to others. This habit eventually became ingrained in my character and core belief system.

> I REALIZED THE NEW VISION OF MY FUTURE FAR OUTWEIGHED ANY FEAR I MAY EXPERIENCE.

Still reveling in the new-found freedom transparency brought into my life, in addition to the progress we had made in bringing wholeness to our marriage, we decided we wanted to help others experience the same. We had come so far from the couple we used to be ... we were no longer those individuals stuck in bitterness, without hope. We wanted to share our success with other couples and encourage them to work through their disappointments. The changes in our marriage had been so drastic that in our naivety we actually felt like we had "arrived" and we were overflowing with the wisdom the world needed to experience as well! It was with this mind-set that we eagerly agreed to attend a two-day conference hosted by Marriage Ministries International (MMI) of Littleton, CO. At that time, MMI did not have an established presence in New York State, so this conference was being conducted with the hopes of not just helping married couples, but also with the vision of identifying and raising up leadership teams to expand its ministry. We attended with the full expectation of becoming leaders in MMI. Were we overconfident? Yes, we absolutely were. Yet we knew the pit of despair God had brought our relationship out from, and couldn't imagine that there was still unresolved issues that needed addressing. We thought we had already reached nirvana.

With great anticipation we made the necessary arrangements to attend the marriage conference. A dear friend offered to watch our three girls for the weekend. Our youngest daughter was only nine months old, so this would be no easy feat. Excitedly, we drove to the conference. We hadn't any more than entered the doors when things began to unravel. Bob had brought cash to pay for the conference, and the people at the registration desk promptly informed us that they did not accept cash. Obviously, going back to our house to get a checkbook or credit card was not an option. Irritated, Bob announced to the registrar, "Fine, we won't be attending if you can't take my cash!" He then turned on his heels and headed for the door. In a state of panic I tried to stop him. It seemed that all was lost before we'd even started! Fortunately, the couple in charge of the event heard the disagreement, came over, and resolved the issue. My body relaxed; we were going to be able to attend after all!

Something had shifted in Bob's attitude, however. He had been offended by their rejection of his hard-earned cash, and was now reluctant to offer them grace. They were going to have to prove their competence to him. I was frustrated at his pride-based attitude, but was still elated and excited that we were attending! I fully expected this conference to further validate what a tremendous job we had done in rescuing our marriage from becoming a divorce statistic. We had worked so hard to get where we were, and I thought this conference would give us the polishing touches we lacked.

The large room was full of couples. In our zeal, we sat near the front. I'm not exactly sure how Bob felt, but I certainly felt like we were God's "star students." Our marriage had been headed for disaster, and against all odds, we had successfully turned it around! I was eager and ready to learn the few missing keys needed to achieve that "perfect" marriage. The seminar started and we were instructed to open our workbooks. It was a bit daunting, but I refused to be discouraged. We had scaled the other mountains, this would seem like a bunny-slope!

Three couples were involved in delivering the presentation. They would weave their personal stories with the text of the workbook. It wasn't long before Bob and I became overwhelmed. It felt like we were immersed in quick-sand. In light of what the Scriptures said about marriage and loving one another, we fell short. Gradually, despair and hopelessness began to replace the excitement we had arrived with. By the time the first day ended, we felt like we were in way over our heads, about to drown. Not only were we discouraged, but we were also very angry. We had gone there expecting to feel like "A" students and left feeling like failures. We both vowed on the way home that we were done! We were not going back for round two; we'd had enough.

Fortunately, by the time we went to bed that evening, we had started to calm down. We began discussing how this conference had cost us nearly one hundred dollars and if we didn't complete it we would not be entitled to even a partial refund. As strange as it seems, that fact alone (plus God's goodness) is what made us decide that despite how miserable we were, we were going back to get our money's worth!

We arrived the next morning on a more somber note than the previous day. Sure enough, it wasn't long before the flood of discouragement and despair threatened to overwhelm us once again. I was furious; I wanted to bolt. I was tired of feeling like a failure when we had worked so hard to succeed. I was angry with Bob, I was angry with the presenting couples and I was also angry at God. The conference was nearing the end as the leaders announced that they would be praying for anyone who would like to come forward. Bob looked at me and asked, "Do you want to go up? I am. I need help or I'm going to give up." I had lost hope, so I responded, "You can go up if you want to, but I'm not." Bob got up and started forward alone. They began to pray for him and I realized I was making a foolish decision. Impulsively, I stood up and nearly ran down the aisle to join Bob.

I don't remember the specific words they prayed for me, but I do know I went from a place of hopelessness to one of hope. Bob had an encounter that forever changed him. As he was being prayed for, he was given a vision, which was not God's usual manner of speaking to him. In this vision, he was running down one corridor after another, brandishing a sword and slaying the enemy. Although greatly outnumbered, it seemed that no foe could stand against him. On and on he fought, successfully making his way toward the escape route. Encouraged by his victories, he went faster and faster, slaying the enemy as he ran. Suddenly, he reached the end of the last corridor, and it was a dead-end. To make matters worse, in front of him stood a HUGE stainless-steel wall, inches thick and too tall to scale. Shocked, he knew he was defeated. He just stood there staring at the impenetrable wall. There was no escape. Suddenly, God spoke to him and said, "You have been winning all kinds of battles by your sheer strength and determination. Your old battle strategies will no longer give you success. From now on, your battles will be won only if you begin to pray with your wife. That is how you will win future battles."

Bob was blown-away by the vision and what God had revealed to him. He went home a changed man. For many years I had tried to get Bob to pray with me, but had never been successful. We prayed at the dinner table over our food, but that was it. He now had a paradigm shift concerning us praying together, and he eagerly initiated it. I reveled in this new-found freedom. We came away from that conference feeling victorious and hopeful. (Being obedient to the Lord's mandate, Bob and I have enjoyed praying together daily for over twenty-five years now!) We felt that MMI was a ministry worth investing in, and undertook the process to become leaders, so we too could share the concepts we learned. Within a year we were leading MMI groups, as much to strengthen our own marriage as to bring hope to others.

TRANSPARENCY LEADS TO VULNERABILITY

Approximately six months after we started leading MMI groups, Bob and I learned another powerful life-lesson. This lesson would be for both of us and would forever mark us as a couple. We learned the power of vulnerability. Webster's Dictionary defines vulnerability as "being capable of being physically wounded; open to attack or damage. Assailable." Upon reading that definition, I doubt it is something that readily appeals to anyone. However, before you decide that this isn't for you, let me explain how this evolved and what a tremendous difference this has made in our lives.

Using the MMI material, we would meet with seven other couples during a thirteen-week period, teaching, leading discussion and praying for individuals or couples at the end of each session. Couples were being positively-impacted and marriages were being healed. We were greatly encouraged. As we began to prepare for the latest thirteen-week study, Bob and I both felt God prompting us to become even more vulnerable and more honest (open) with the couples we were facilitating. It wasn't that we weren't doing these things with the couples before... we just weren't as completely vulnerable and open as we might have been with the information we shared. We would conveniently leave out specific details that might incriminate us (or others) when recounting a story. I doubt people would initially be excited to have God tell you to be more vulnerable; we were no exception.

Many of the topics covered during the thirteen weeks of MMI were areas in which we had experienced victory in our own marriage. Therefore, we were able to teach the studies from personal experience, making the groups a lot more interesting than just following a study-guide alone. If the week's topic was forgiveness, I could tell the story of marital unfaithfulness. I would relate how I had been unfaithful to Bob early in our marriage, and had finally worked up the courage to confess to him and our pastor. I would then describe how God had miraculously put it on Bob's heart to forgive both myself and the man I was involved with. You would have to actually know Bob to understand what a miracle that in itself was! Of course, by the time we told this story we were several weeks into the study, so the group did know Bob and were impressed with what God had done. Everyone in the room believed that if God did this for us, He could do it for them as well. Therefore, the stories became a crucial part of the study.

Each week was a different lesson and we would have a relevant story to share. It was always exciting, never a dull moment. However, as we told our stories, we were deliberately vague, not giving too much detail, and certainly not giving specifics that might later be used as evidence against us! We told enough of the story to get the point across and to impart hope, but we were not being totally vulnerable. We protected ourselves and it seemed prudent to do this. Plus, it felt more COMFORTABLE to be guarded! We told our stories, had lots of laughs, opportunities to pray with others, and we never felt threatened or uncomfortable. It seemed like a "win-win" to us.

That is, until one evening while sharing a particular story, I suddenly got a strong impression that we were supposed to tell the WHOLE story! I felt God urging me to include some of the important details that really showcased His amazing power. In other words, to be 100% honest and VULNERABLE! Yikes! I promptly ignored His prompting—I did NOT want to be obedient—but as the night went on I could not shake the feeling. I leaned over to Bob and whispered what God was prompting me to tell, asking him if he agreed? His face turned a few shades of gray. He told me later that all he could think was "Oh great! Not only do we live in this small community where everyone knows everyone else, but this is going to ruin our small business, as no one will want to have anything to do with us after this!" Yet, he too had a sense that it was the right thing to do, so he nodded in approval. Later, he told me that when he became fearful of being so vulnerable, God clearly spoke to his heart and asked, "Are you willing to sacrifice your reputation to accomplish My purpose in people and set them free?" Immediately, his heart answered "Yes!" At that moment we had no idea how this decision would profoundly change not only us, but everyone associated with us from that time forward.

> "ARE YOU WILLING TO SACRIFICE YOUR REPUTATION TO ACCOMPLISH MY PURPOSE TO SET THEM FREE?"

The topic that week was forgiveness. When Bob nodded, giving me permission to be vulnerable, I knew I needed to tell this group how things had really unfolded, instead of the sanitized version we had presented in the past. I began to relay the story of the marital unfaithfulness described in the previous chapter. When we had previously shared this story, we had always discussed Bob's infidelity, my devastating plan of revenge which resulted in additional adultery, and the two times I confessed my unfaithfulness to Bob. How he immediately forgave me the first time, but did not respond so readily the second time. Because the individual I had committed adultery with lived in the area, we had never given any details of how difficult it was for Bob to work through the issue of forgiveness after I had rekindled the affair. Now, however, I knew God wanted us to tell the story, so others could relate to it and possibly apply it to their own lives. It was of utmost importance to us, however, that this man remain anonymous, as vulnerability does not give one permission to expose and harm others.

Years before I had ever committed adultery, Bob would periodically say that if he ever found out I was unfaithful to him, he would kill the guy. He had miraculously forgiven me the first time I had confessed to him, but I was more apprehensive about having to tell him the second time. Although I didn't think he would really carry out his threat, I wasn't totally sure. I had witnessed his temper in action several times, and I knew he was certainly strong enough to carry out his threat if he wanted to... so, there was a huge risk in telling him. I had already created enough of a mess, I didn't want additional carnage!

Upon confessing my adultery to Bob the second time, I immediately felt better. It was as if a huge weight had been lifted from my shoulders as the truth came to light. Bob, on the other hand, felt like his world had come crashing in. He started rehashing the past times that had seemed "suspicious" between our mutual friend and myself, but had disregarded it not only because he trusted me, but he trusted this man as well. Over and over he would hear the self-tormenting accusation, *"I can't believe what a fool I was! I actually trusted him and he betrayed me! He deserves to suffer for the betrayal!"* His days were now consumed with two continuous thoughts: should he exact his revenge or let God work things out as He seemed to promise in his Word? He mentally rehearsed various ways of injuring this man he had once considered a close friend, and Bob's sense of justice seemed to affirm these actions. He knew he didn't want to kill him, just injure him badly enough to hospitalize the man, thereby giving him plenty of time for reflection of his sin. However, before Bob took any action, God's presence would once again bring wisdom, and he eventually abandoned those vengeful thoughts. A couple of times God literally restrained Bob as he was preparing to confront this man. Of course, I never knew this until several years later, but was aware of the huge chasm between us.

Forgiveness became a huge stumbling block for Bob. It seemed that he would work through the issue of forgiving our friend, believing it was fully resolved, only to have the tormenting thoughts return. *"I am a fool to let this guy get away with the betrayal."* Initially Bob lived with this inner struggle on a moment-by-moment basis, but as the weeks turned into months, it became less frequent. Bob told me years later the only thing that kept him from acting on his impulses was his habit of listening to the Word of God on cassette. Whenever he was working at home or driving his truck he would listen to Scripture. When he would dwell on the irrational thoughts, it would be God's Word that brought him back to reality. My ex-lover had no idea I had confessed to Bob, nor did he have any idea how many times God had protected him by restraining Bob from acting impetuously.

There was also one very specific story in the Bible that really spoke to Bob's heart. It was the story of David and Nabal found in the book of 1 Samuel 25:1-3:

"Then Samuel died; and the Israelites gathered together and lamented for him, and buried him at his home in Ramah. And David arose and went down to the Wilderness of Paran. Now there was a man in Maon whose business was in Carmel, and the man was very rich. He had three thousand sheep and a thousand goats. And he was shearing his sheep in Carmel. The name of the man was Nabal, and the name of his wife was Abigail. And she was a woman of good understanding and beautiful appearance; but the man was harsh and evil in his doings. He was of the house of Caleb.

When David heard in the wilderness that Nabal was shearing his sheep, David sent ten young men, "Go up to Carmel, go to Nabal, and greet him in my name. And thus you shall say to him who lives in prosperity: 'Peace be to you, peace to your house, and peace to all that you have. Now I have heard that you have shearers. Your shepherds were with us, and we did not hurt them, nor was there anything missing from them all the while they were in Carmel. Ask your young men, and they will tell you. Therefore let my young men find favor in your eyes, for we come on a feast day. Please give whatever comes to your hand to your servants and to your son David.'" So when David's young men came, they spoke to Nabal according to all these words in the name of David, and waited.

Then Nabal answered David's servants, and said, "Who is David, and who is the son of Jesse? There are many servants nowadays who break away each one from his master. Shall I then take my bread and my water and my meat that I have killed for my shearers, and give it to men when I do not know where they are from?" So David's young men turned on their heels and went back; and they came and told him all these words. Then David said to his men, "Every man gird on his sword." So every man girded on his sword. And about four hundred men went with David, and two hundred stayed with the supplies.

Now one of the young men told Abigail, Nabal's wife, saying, "Look, David sent messengers from the wilderness to greet our master; and he reviled them. But the men were very good to us, and we were not hurt, nor did we miss anything as long as we accompanied them, when we were in the fields. They were a wall to us both by night and day, all the time we were with them keeping the sheep. Now therefore, know and consider what you will do, for harm is determined against our master and against all his household. For he is such a scoundrel that one cannot speak to him." Then Abigail made haste and took two hundred loaves of bread, two skins of wine, five sheep already dressed, five seahs of roasted grain, one hundred clusters of raisins, and two hundred cakes of figs, and loaded them on donkeys. And she said to her servants, "Go on before me; see, I am coming after you." But she did not tell her husband Nabal.

So it was, as she rode on the donkey, that she went down under cover of the hill; and there were David and his men, coming down toward her, and she met them. Now David had said, "Surely in vain I have protected all that this fellow has in the wilderness, so that nothing was missed of all that belongs to him. And he has repaid me evil for good. May God do so, and more also, to the enemies of David, if I leave one male of all who belong to him by morning light."

Now when Abigail saw David, she dismounted quickly from the donkey, fell on her face before David, and bowed down to the ground. So she fell at his feet and said: "On me, my lord, on me let this iniquity be! And please let your maidservant speak in your ears, and hear the words of your maidservant. Please, let not my lord regard this scoundrel Nabal. For as his name is, so is he: Nabal is his name, and folly is with him! But

I, your maidservant, did not see the young men of my lord whom you sent. Now therefore, my lord, as the LORD lives and as your soul lives, since the LORD has held you back from coming to bloodshed and from avenging yourself with your own hand, now then, let your enemies and those who seek harm for my lord be as Nabal. And now this present which your maidservant has brought to my lord, let it be given to the young men who follow my lord. Please forgive the trespass of your maidservant. For the LORD will certainly make for my lord an enduring house, because my lord fights the battles of the LORD, and evil is not found in you throughout your days. Yet a man has risen to pursue you and seek your life, but the life of my lord shall be bound in the bundle of the living with the LORD your God; and the lives of your enemies He shall sling out , as from the pocket of a sling. And it shall come to pass, when the LORD has done for my lord according to all the good that He has spoken concerning you, and has appointed you ruler over Israel, that this will be no grief to you, nor offense of heart to my lord, wither that you have shed blood without cause, or that my lord has avenged himself.

"But when the LORD has dealt well with my lord, then remember your maidservant." Then David said to Abigail: "Blessed is the LORD God of Israel, who sent you this day to meet me! And blessed is your advice and blessed are you, because you have kept me this day from coming to bloodshed and from avenging myself with my own hand. For indeed, as the LORD God of Israel lives, who has kept me back from hurting

you, unless you had hurried and come to meet me, surely by morning light no males would have been left to Nabal!"

So David received from her hand what she had brought him, and said to her, "Go up in peace to your house. See, I have heeded your voice and respected your person." Now Abigail went to Nabal, and there he was, holding a feast in his house, like a feast of a king. And Nabal's heart was merry within him, for he was very drunk; therefore she told him nothing, little or much, until morning light. So it was, in the morning, when the wind had gone from Nabal, and his wife had told him these things, that his heart died within him, and he became like a stone. Then it happened, after about ten days, that the LORD struck Nabal, and he died."

In Scripture, David gives thanks to God for restraining his hand and keeping him from committing the sin of harming Nabal and his family. 1 Samuel 25:39a says, *"So when David heard that Nabal was dead, he said, 'Blessed be the LORD, who has pleaded the cause of my reproach from the hand of Nabal, and has kept His servant from evil!'"* It was this last verse that really pierced Bob's heart. He realized, that just like David, he too had wanted to seek revenge by his own hand. However, as with David, it would be evil in the sight of God. Bob would repeatedly counsel himself with this Scripture whenever vengeful thoughts would return. As he continued to counsel himself, his heart began to align with God and His Word.

OBEDIENCE BRINGS RELEASE

Several years passed, and the issue of true forgiveness towards this man finally seemed to be actualized. Our marriage was experiencing great healing as well and this facilitated the process. Understandably, Bob had avoided contact with his ex-friend, but eventually started stopping by his house, visiting with him and eventually re-establishing their close friendship. Bob hadn't really planned this, he just felt it was the right thing to do. I was aware of this, and was amazed at the freedom Bob was experiencing. I had little contact with the man, as I felt that was the wisest choice.

Unbeknownst to me, however, Bob had a plan of dealing with this betrayal and solidifying his forgiveness once and for all. It was mid-winter, and the ground was covered with a fresh snowfall. Bob called him and asked if he would like to help him clear a cross-country ski trail with their machetes. The friend readily agreed as the three of us had done a lot of skiing together in the past and had many fond memories of these times. I had no idea that Bob had an agenda, so I thought nothing of it. Bob sharpened his machete as he waited for our friend to arrive.

Bob later told me what had transpired in the woods. The two of them had been cutting brush with their machetes for about an hour when Bob suddenly quit cutting, turned around to face him, and with machete in hand, said, "I know what you did with my wife." He said the man's face turned as white as the snow-cover. If it had been me, I think I would have fainted from fear! Bob then calmly said, "I just want you to know that I forgive you. All I want is for you to get your life right with God." As you can imagine, it was a defining moment for them both. I don't know what else transpired in their conversation, but Bob came back home knowing that it was finally settled; unforgiveness no longer had any power over his life or our marriage.

It would be days before Bob spoke of what had happened on that ski trail. I could tell that a huge burden had been lifted from his shoulders. In addition, he was relieved that there was no longer any deception between him and his friend – it was true restoration.

Not long after this, we were praying with another friend. Spontaneously, Bob prayed, "God, thank you for the faithful wife you have given me." To tell you the truth, I didn't hear the rest of his prayer. Tears were streaming down my cheeks and thankfulness was overflowing in my heart. I knew that God had so changed my heart that I would never again be unfaithful to our marriage vows, but I wasn't sure that Bob knew that ... I had already decided that I was not going to tell him of the change in my heart. Talk is cheap. I had decided to let my actions reveal the truth over time, regardless of how long it would take. So, when he prayed that prayer nearly five years after I had initially confessed my infidelity to him, I knew how significant it was! God had done a complete healing; not just in my heart, but in Bob's as well!

This was the story we told the marriage group after God had told us to be vulnerable. It was real, raw and full of emotion, and it contained enough detail for people to relate to on an emotional level. It was no longer the sanitized version of forgiveness that we had previously shared with the marriage groups. The response from the group was shocking. Some cried, others were silent, all were deeply impacted. They could relate it to areas of their own lives where forgiveness was needed. One after another, the individuals began to relate their personal stories and deal with the unresolved and buried issues that had been present for years. It was phenomenal. Bob and I just listened in shock, never realizing what an avalanche of freedom our obedience would release in the group!

Vulnerability is defined as "capable of being physically wounded; open to attack or damage, and assailable." Choosing to be vulnerable that evening was a risk, however God immediately demonstrated to us that when we trust Him with our reputation, great things can happen! We were sold! We decided then and there that it was worth the risk!

Once in a great while we will deliberately choose **not** to be vulnerable or transparent with an individual, but this is certainly the exception and not the rule. If we sense that the person is ill-intentioned or has an agenda, we will choose to keep the conversation somewhat limited. Again, this is most definitely the exception to the rule. We have found that vulnerability is a huge blessing, not only for us, but for others as well. As I alluded to earlier, it is very important to protect another's story while being vulnerable and transparent. I have the right to be open and honest about my life, but I do not have the right to expose details about another's without their permission. It is extremely important to use discretion when relating an experience involving other individuals.

Vulnerability has become a bedrock value for Bob and me. If an acquaintance or friend is asked to describe us, *vulnerable* and *transparent* will often be the first adjectives they use. It has blessed our relationships, and it has created a safe place for others when they are with us. We do not struggle with what to tell a person or what not to; we have learned to be ourselves. We are comfortable with who we are, and that allows others to be comfortable in our presence as well. Before you know it, they are modeling the same vulnerability and transparency in their own lives, and we are all richer for it. Our closets are "clean," there are no skeletons hidden here. There is nothing from our past or present shrouded in darkness. Therefore, we do not live in fear of what others may learn about us, and I no longer fear being exposed by others. Such freedom! We have chosen to do our best to live in the light, and have given our reputation to the Lord for Him to use for His glory.

My relationships are my most valued possessions. Whereas I use to strive to develop meaningful relationships, they now come naturally and easily. Vulnerability and transparency have been huge factors in this. It enables me to get to know people very quickly and to develop deep friendships with them because there are no walls between us. Have some people been intimidated or turned-off by my approach to life? I'm sure there are a few. But I have learned to have grace even for those that are offended. More times than not, these offended individuals are hiding behind their own masks. Although they may be initially scared or offended, I have learned that most everyone has a deep desire to be fully known and seen for who they truly are. I am thrilled when a person living behind the control of a mask dares to abandon it and walk in freedom! I can't help but rejoice with them, knowing what amazing blessings their future holds!

PRAYER FOR CHOOSING TO REMOVE THE MASK

Heavenly Father, when Jesus walked this earth He modeled transparency and vulnerability for all to see. He was able to relate to others freely and openly. Father, that is the desire of my heart. I want the freedom and confidence to be true to myself. To be comfortable with who I really am. I am so tired of trying to perform to please others. I am so tired of pretending to be someone other than who I am. I see the blessings of transparency and vulnerability and I want it to be part of my life.

Father, I ask that You would first deal with the fear. I admit that the thought of being fully transparent and vulnerable is scary. Right now, Father, I choose to break the fear of man off my life. I admit that I have been more concerned with pleasing people than pleasing You... I repent of that and I ask Your forgiveness. Thank You Father, that by the blood of Jesus I am washed whiter than snow. Your Word says that perfect love casts out all fear, so right now I ask that where fear once gripped my heart that You would now come and fill me with Your perfect love. Thank you Father for Your tangible love. As I quiet myself before You, would you speak to me? Would You share Your heart with me and tell me what You think of me? How special I am to You? Thank you, Daddy.

Abba, I ask that You would now give me courage to deal with anything that I have hidden in my closet. I no longer want to live with the skeletons of my past controlling my life and causing me to live in fear. I want to walk in freedom, so I give You permission to search it out. I choose to deal with each and every item that You show me. Show me, Father.

I come into agreement with You that this will no longer have any power over my life. I choose to bring it OUT of the closet into your Glorious Light and will deal with it as you direct. All power that it once had I now break off by the power of the blood of Jesus. Thank you!

Now, Father, I choose to come into agreement with You and Your Word. Your Word says,"Who the Son sets free is free indeed." I thank You for that. I choose to walk in that freedom. I choose to truly love and help others instead of being afraid of them. No longer will I be afraid of what they might think of me. I choose to only fear You, God: to love what You love and hate what You hate. You and You alone will I fear. You will be my guide; You will be my standard. I will walk in Your love. Amaze me, God, with the freedom that will come into my life from these decisions! Let it bring freedom not just to my life, but also to all those that I come into contact with. Amen.

FOUR

LEAVING CHANCE BEHIND
CHOOSING TO BE INTENTIONAL

"Growth is the great separator between those who succeed and those who do not. When I see a person beginning to separate themselves from the pack, it's almost always due to growth."

JOHN C. MAXWELL

"The secret of your success is determined by your daily agenda."

JOHN C. MAXWELL

A few years ago we were leading a small group using John C. Maxwell's book *The 15 Invaluable Laws of Growth*. At the end of each chapter were life questions to answer introspectively. I will never forget one week's assignment in particular. It was week three and the chapter was "The Law of the Mirror: You Must See Value in Yourself to Add Value to Yourself." The first application question challenged the reader to spend several days making a list of your best one hundred (yes, one hundred!) personal characteristics. After making the list of one hundred strengths, the next assignment was to decide which single trait best describes you... a daunting exercise to be sure, but also life-changing for almost everyone in the group! When all was said and done, the one word that best described me was "INTENTIONAL!" I have not always been that person. As a matter of fact, if you asked anyone who knew me before my mid-thirties they would tell you I was reckless, flew by the seat of my pants, and had little direction for my life. I was not in charge of my life; I was reactive, and my circumstances were in charge of me!

It all began to change a few years after I learned that love was more than an emotion. God started to impress upon Bob and me that we needed to be intentional about the direction our lives were taking. It wasn't that we were headed in what many people would consider a *bad* direction—or that we were doing anything terribly wrong ... it was just that we weren't being *intentional*. We left too much to chance. There were areas of our lives that did display planning and self-discipline, as we usually read the Bible, regularly attended a Bible study and church service, embodied great work ethic and had good jobs. The rest of our life, however, we seemed to leave to chance. What God was impressing on our hearts now seemed different and required a paradigm shift. We were leading marriage studies, but felt that in order to impact more people, we needed our own personal growth. Where were we to start? We had no idea.

Shortly thereafter, I saw an announcement for an upcoming John C. Maxwell leadership conference. I immediately knew this is where we were to begin. Bob and I agreed that I would go alone and "check it out." I quickly realized that it was God who had led me there, and He had a plan and a purpose! Maxwell talked about personal growth, and gave very practical ways to make it a reality. It was just what we needed! I felt like we had been wandering through the desert and had stumbled upon a lush oasis! I was hooked. I excitedly called Bob and we decided that I should buy the materials to start our growth plan.

Since God was specifically wanting us to grow in our personal leadership skills, that was the material I focused on. I left the conference with a zeal to change, and the resources to make it reality. We decided that our growth plan would include reading one leadership book a month, listening to two associated cassette tapes per week (there were no CD's when we first started), and attend at least one leadership conference per year. We were incredibly hungry and it felt like God had brought us to the banquet table! Most of the information we were reading and listening to was completely foreign to us, so we would often have to listen to the same cassette tape several times in order to fully grasp what was being taught. The same applied to the books—we would often have to read sections over and over again to grasp the content. We were far from discouraged, however. We were hungry and loving every minute of it.

The initial investment seemed a bit overwhelming, as I left that first seminar with a year's supply of resources valued at over five hundred dollars. However, it wasn't long before we started to see a return on our investment. We started incorporating many of the leadership skills we learned, and within a short time we noticed some huge changes. Our communication skills were increasing, we had more ideas and options when helping individuals, and they were experiencing greater success. Coupled with this, we had learned and adopted servant-leadership as a lifestyle, and we were loving all it entailed. As we actively served those around us, putting their needs before ours, we noticed that our effectiveness and influence greatly increased. People sensed that we genuinely cared about them, and therefore trusted us when we imparted solid advice. A beautiful cycle began to emerge in our lives that continues to this day. As we incorporated what we learned, it gave us the opportunity to use the leadership skills to bless others and help them succeed. We were loving that God was actually giving us the opportunity to put the principles into practice. This fueled our hunger even more!

QUIT HANGING AROUND LOSERS

Eventually God began to impress upon us that we needed to be intentional in another area of our lives, one that we had deliberately avoided: our friendships. Years prior, when Bob and I attended the marriage retreat weekend where I had initially confessed my adultery to him, an internationally known prophet had prayed for us. We were so new in the faith that we had not even known that there were modern-day prophets in the church! After he had spoken one evening, I said to Bob, "I think we are supposed to have him pray for us!" We were so naïve that we had no idea what to expect, or even if we should expect anything at all! As we approached the prophet, I assumed he would first gather some personal information from us ... instead, he immediately took hold of our hands, asked us our names, and began to pray!

I was a skeptic, and it was as if God knew it and wanted me to feel confident He was in this. Immediately the prophet told us about five very specific circumstances we had been praying about. No one (other than Bob and I) knew of these five situations. Maybe I should rephrase that ... No one except Bob, myself, and GOD! The prophet rattled-off all five items, first telling us what we had prayed about, and then telling us how God specifically wanted us to deal with each situation! It was shocking to say the least, and by the time he was done, God clearly had our attention! We felt dazed by all that had been revealed, and as quickly as the prophet had started praying, he quit. He let go of our hands, and we walked away. We had only gone 20 feet when we heard the prophet's voice calling loudly over the crowd. "Hey! Hey you! You young couple! Stop! Turn around!" We couldn't imagine it was us being addressed ... as just about every young couple in the room turned toward the voice. We looked, and there he was, pointing his finger at us, trying to get our attention. He then said, "God has one more message for you: "Quit hanging around losers! You hear? You, I'm talking to you, young man! Quit hanging around losers!"

We instinctively knew what God was talking about. First Corinthians 15:33 says, *"Stop fooling yourselves! Evil companions will corrupt good morals and character"* (TPT). It wasn't that our friends were *evil* by the world's standards; they were still living the same wild and unrestrained lifestyle that we had lived prior to our conversion to Christ. Now, however, we found ourselves torn between two different realities ... we had new friends that were Christians, but still hung out with our old friends as well, because we enjoyed the risqué adventures they were involved in.

It was clear that we had to make a change. Our hearts told us we couldn't live in both worlds, but emotionally we didn't want to make the break. After hearing the prophetic word hurled across the room, it was obvious that the time had come for us to make a decision. We returned home from that conference being much more conscious of who we spent time with. Because we were very young in the faith, we interpreted the prophetic message to mean that our friendships were to be with only Christians. That single parameter became our new standard. To our surprise, we learned that there were lots of people that called themselves "Christians" but whose lifestyle was not all that different from our old friends. However, as long as they called themselves "Christians" we didn't question it.

> OUR HEARTS TOLD US WE COULDN'T LIVE IN BOTH WORLDS, BUT EMOTIONALLY WE DIDN'T WANT TO MAKE THE BREAK.

It would be years later on our personal growth plan that God would once again address this area of our lives. We attended a second John C. Maxwell leadership conference and he stated with assurance that he could reliably predict what a person's life would look like in five years simply by observing the people they hung around with, the movies they watched, and the books they read. This statement may have over-simplified the issue, but we got the point! Although we were now intentionally reading books on self-improvement, we realized we were not very selective about the movies we watched, and had never been fully obedient regarding God's directive to intentionally choose with whom we associated. The movies were an easy problem to solve. However, dealing with relationships was a bit more complicated.

YOUR FRIENDS ARE INFLUENCERS

Maxwell challenged each attendee to intentionally choose our influencers, his point being that friends can determine the path of our future. My initial response to that admonition was to argue with it ... surely I could be friends with whomever I wished! I resisted the change. I rationalized that my friends were not influencing or affecting my future in any way! However I could not stop thinking about his bold statement. I had to admit that those I considered my closest friends were also the ones I spent the most time with, even seeking advice from them. Whether I wanted to admit it or not, they did influence my life, and were charting the course of my future, whether I intended it or not! I liked my friends, even loved them, but that did not mean that I wanted my life to mirror theirs ... Maxwell's comment haunted me. Knowing he possessed more life-experience and people-skills than I made me realize it would be foolish not to take his admonition to heart.

I instinctively knew that the winds of change were blowing into our relationships and this area was going to require some pruning! There was an apparent dichotomy in our lives: we wanted to serve God and experience personal growth, yet we did not hang around people that fostered it. Maxwell once said, "Eventually, you must disengage from the relationships you've outgrown, or they will limit your growth as a leader." Unfortunately, many of our friends had no interest in any kind of intentional personal growth, certainly not in the direction that God seemed to be directing Bob and me. As a matter of fact, most of our friends just wanted us to continue being the people they had always known, and forget about changing altogether! They didn't like the changes we were making, and often ridiculed us for it. A chasm was opening, and we seemed to have no control over it. In reality, we did have control over it; we could choose to stop growing and changing... but that option was unacceptable.

We started asking God to bring new friends into our lives. We desired friends that would not only accept us, but also encourage us to think bigger and grow to become all we could be. We were now ready to be intentional in this area of our lives as well, yet were initially unsure of how to proceed. We started observing people's lives. We looked for people that were either traveling in the same direction we were, or were far ahead of us. When we would meet a person displaying this, we would often be attracted to them and a friendship would emerge. Other times we would actually approach people, tell them of our growth plan and desire to change, and ask them if they would be willing to spend time with us as mentors. More often than not, the people we approached would agree to help us out in one way or another. Some individuals recommended books for us to read, some agreed to meet with us weekly or biweekly, others imparted to us whenever their schedules allowed. We were so eager and hungry to learn that we did whatever we had to do to make it work. We didn't demand that they fit into our schedule. Instead, we did everything we could to fit into theirs.

Amazing changes began to occur. First of all, it was apparent that some of these people we had invited into our circle would become cherished life-long friends. We loved spending time with them! They challenged and encouraged us to become all that we were designed to be. We enjoyed each other's company as we journeyed together towards our God-given destinies. Some of the people could only mentor us for a season, as they were busy. However, as one person would leave our circle, God would miraculously allow another to enter in. He was teaching us about quality in relationships. We were amazed at the depth of intimacy we were experiencing and thoroughly enjoying this journey!

The vast number of true friends we have gained through this process is absolutely mind-blowing. We consider each and everyone of them a treasure, and have consistently tried to bless them as they have blessed us. We never imagined that our lives would be blessed by so many true, faithful friends! Now, more than twenty years after we first began deliberately choosing our friendships and influencers, I remain profoundly grateful. Whereas initially we resisted this change, I now see how greatly it has impacted our lives and the lives of countless others!

> INITIALLY WE RESISTED THIS CHANGE—I NOW SEE HOW GREATLY IT HAS IMPACTED OUR LIVES!

So, you might wonder, what ever happened to those friends that we deliberately removed from our inner circle at the beginning of this journey? Did we throw them away like rubbish and just forget about them? Absolutely not! Although we limited the time we spent with them, we were careful not to destroy the relationship or make them feel rejected. The most surprising thing happened with many of these individuals. Whereas they used to influence us, we now have the honor and privilege of influencing many of **them**. They have witnessed our growth first-hand and, as a result, they often sought us out for advice when their life-choices led to turbulence in their lives. We've been able to share life-changing principles with them, and encourage them as they walk through hardships. It has changed many of their lives. A few of them have even initiated their own deliberate growth plan! We do whatever we can to support, encourage, and invest in their journey. Some of these individuals have transformed their personal lives, and we have returned to being extremely close friends. Others we see occasionally...we love and value these people and do what we can to help in their journey.

KEY #4—INTENTIONAL GROWTH IS A CHOICE

When God first impressed on our hearts to start being deliberate and intentional in our actions and decisions twenty years ago, we had no idea how greatly it would impact our life. It has changed not only us, but also the lives of those we have the honor and privilege of associating with. Being deliberate and intentional has become a way of life for us. Everywhere we go we are looking to see what our Heavenly Father is doing so we can be a part of it. We don't take any encounter for granted; we believe God has a purpose in everything we do, every day. We believe He has set divine appointments up for us, daily situations, in which He wants us to partner with Him. Therefore, we live in such a way that we are constantly seeking His guidance and leadership. We no longer live by chance; we have left that behind! Our lives are now filled with destiny and the gratification that only comes from KNOWING that you are doing exactly what you were created to do! There is nothing more fulfilling than walking fully in your identity and destiny; that is God's heart for each and every one of us!

It makes me shudder to think back to the time when we had no growth plan, no direction, and no filter with regard to who was influencing and impacting our lives. We had initially decided to make those changes simply out of obedience to what we felt the Father was speaking into our hearts. If we had ever had the privilege of glimpsing into our future and seeing the tremendous benefits of it, we would have eagerly jumped in with both feet many years earlier!

It is never too late to change! It doesn't matter what your age is, how many mistakes you have made, or how badly you think you have messed up. God has created an amazing destiny and purpose for each of us ... His heart's desire is that we enter into it. It's an adventure full of excitement, reward, and satisfaction. And, as if that isn't enough, the AMAZING

IT IS NEVER TOO
LATE TO CHANGE!

BEFORE YOU KNOW
IT, THE FUTURE
WILL BE BRIGHTER.

life-long relationships you make along the way are so incredible! All it requires is that you live deliberately. Ask God which area of your life He would like to start with, develop a growth plan that supports it, and ask people who have had success in that area come along-side you. Before you know it, the future will be brighter. New and greater opportunities will be presented to you, and you will be having the time of your life!

PRAYER FOR CHOOSING
TO BE INTENTIONAL

Heavenly Father, I realize and admit that I have not stewarded my life and my calling as intentionally as I should have... I repent, and ask that You would forgive me. I choose this day to change. I choose to embrace this day as a new beginning.

I thank You Father that I have a hope and a future. That I am not on this earth just to wander aimlessly. I have a destiny and a purpose. I have been created to fulfill a calling that only I can fulfill! I want to be the best I can be. Father, I no longer want to live a haphazard life with little or no direction. I want to be like an arrow, shot forth out of Your bow, destined to hit the target and accomplish its purpose.

Father, from this day forward I choose to deliberately and intentionally partner with You so I can do this. In areas of my life that need to be pruned and adjusted, I give you permission to do what You know is best for me. I trust You, Father. In areas where I need to grow, I ask Father that You would help me to design a very practical growth plan that can become a lifestyle for me. I also ask that You would bring leaders around me to encourage me. Bring people into my life that can walk with me, and help me to grow.

Father, I ask right now that You would give me a glimpse of how You see me. Give me a glimpse of what You created me for, a glimpse of the hope and the future that You have for me. Your word says that without vision your people perish, so Father I am asking for vision... give me a vision that is bigger than myself. A vision of who I was meant to be and how that will impact the world around me. Thank You, Father.

I choose right now to partner with that vision. I choose to fully embrace my calling and my destiny. Father, I choose right now to engage with You and do what I need to do to make it happen. I choose: YES! Yes, I will prepare. Yes, I will deliberately and intentionally grow so I can impact the world for Your Kingdom! Yes, I will do what I can do, God, so You can do what only YOU can do! I rebuke all lethargy and choose this day to fully embrace whatever it is I need to do to become trained and prepared. Thank you Father, for choosing ME to be a world-changer! Amen.

FIVE

PARENTING WITHOUT AN IDENTITY CRISIS

CHOOSING TO SEPARATE YOUR KID'S MISTAKES FROM YOUR IDENTITY

"A man (woman) must be big enough to admit his (her) mistakes, smart enough to profit from them, and strong enough to correct them."

JOHN C. MAXWELL

We had never planned on being bad parents; as a matter of fact, we had never planned on being parents at all. For the first ten years that Bob and I were together, we were selfish individuals. We knew that about ourselves, and strangely enough, we were okay with it. We loved having no one else to care for, and no one demanding anything of us that we didn't want to give. We realized that this was not an ideal environment to raise children in, and therefore decided that children would not be a part of our future. Watching in amazement as parents attempted to interact with their unruly children reinforced our decision. We could not for the life of us figure out how a thirty-pound child could render a grown adult so helpless. In our hearts we judged the parents as weak and impotent. It was beyond our comprehension. *Surely*, we thought, *parenting can't be THAT difficult!*

With hearts full of judgment, Bob and I agreed that if we were to ever have children (which we were sure would **never** happen!) we wouldn't be THAT KIND of parent! We would be GOOD parents, able to control our kids. They would be perfectly behaved and well disciplined. As a matter of fact, we wouldn't just be good parents, we would be GREAT parents! Little did we know that we were setting ourselves up for disaster. We were unaware of the wisdom shared in Matthew 7:1-2, *"Refuse to be a critic full of bias toward others, and judgment will not be passed on you. For you'll be judged by the same standard that you've used to judge others. The measurement you use on them will be used on you"* (TPT). Had we taken that verse to heart, we would have been more circumscribed in our criticism of those parents.

To our surprise, a few years after we committed our lives to Christ, our hearts began to soften. Through unforeseen circumstances, we ended up getting involved with our church youth group. To our surprise we actually loved and **enjoyed** these teenagers! It was great doing wild and crazy activities with them and we valued the relationships we were developing. Our age difference was just enough so that we were role models for them, yet we were young enough to keep up with their physical activities. *Wow*, we thought, *life doesn't get much better than this ... maybe we really DO like kids!* It certainly didn't look like parenting these teens was a big deal! Of course, we had no concept of what these parents might be dealing with at home; we had no frame of reference. Perhaps God was using our naivete for our good. Within a couple of years we began entertaining the idea of having our own family and before we knew it, we started planning for it.

What we did not take into consideration was how utterly unprepared we were for this task. Bob and I had never babysat, never changed a baby's diaper, nor even held a baby! For that matter, neither of us had ever *wanted* to hold a baby! Clearly this had all the signs of a disaster in the making, but we were blind to it. We simply didn't know what we didn't know... but, in our overconfidence, we plowed forward and dove in. Many of our peers who had young children thought it was a great idea for us to join them in the adventure of parenting. Others tried to gently warn us that perhaps we didn't know what we were getting into, but we were deaf to their wisdom. We were absolutely confident that we were going to be great parents. No, PERFECT parents! After all, how hard could it be?

It wasn't long before we were pregnant with our first daughter, Sarah. Two weeks prior to Sarah's birth, a friend (apparently possessing more wisdom than I), invited me to her house to inform me of what we might expect and need after we brought our baby home from the hospital. She was horrified at my ignorance and rightly so. I was clueless. Poor Sarah was going to be our little human guinea pig.

BEST PARENTS *EVER!*

There should be parenting classes for people like us, and maybe there are, but I was unaware of any. Unfortunately, in many aspects, Sarah ended up being our teacher instead of the other way around. Regardless, we remained convinced we were going to be the best parents ever. I even quit my job in pharmaceutical research after Sarah's birth so I could be a stay-at-home mom ... we were going to do this RIGHT. Sarah (and subsequent children) were going to be perfect, constant sources of joy, and people that, even at a young age, would change the world forever!

Without realizing what was happening within our hearts, Bob and I were already beginning to integrate our personal success and the behavior of our children. We were beginning to allow our identities to be dictated by something (and someone) other than God. Without ever meaning to, our belief system could be summarized as: if our child(ren) behaved, we looked good and were therefore successful! Our self-worth and identities unfortunately became intertwined with their behavior. It was a very subtle shift and it would be many years before we would be able to put a voice to what happened, yet it was there all the same.

Within five years we had three beautiful daughters. Jamie, our middle daughter, was born when Sarah was 3 ½ years old, and April followed 18 months later. It wasn't long before we realized parenting was a bit more complicated than we had initially imagined. Chaos became the norm. I seemed to run out of energy before I ran out of tasks needing to be finished. Still, I struggled to maintain the appearance of our "perfect" little family. Of course, things were NOT perfect! The girls fought and squabbled as all children do. Teaching them right from wrong seemed exhausting with very little reward, and they could make messes faster than I could clean them! I felt like a failure.

SELF-DECEPTION IS A POWERFUL FORCE

Allowing my self-worth and self-image to be directly tied to parenting created a recipe for disaster. I was caught on a hamster wheel, so oblivious I had no idea that I needed to get off! If the girls were doing great, it meant I was a great mom. If they were perfect, it meant I was perfect, if they were well-liked and accepted, I was accepted as well. On and on it went. However, it actually went much deeper than that. It didn't mean that I was just accepted as a mom, doing great as a mom, or was perfect as a mom. It meant that as a PERSON I was accepted, great, and perfect! My entire *identity* was yoked to parenting! As long as they looked good to the world, I was as a good person. But as soon as they publicly misbehaved in any way, as all children do, I came undone. I felt worthless, rejected, lacking, insignificant, and a thousand other emotions that would speak death to my fragile ego and identity.

The girls were no longer free to be normal little kids. Unbeknownst to them, there was an unspoken code stating that they were responsible for determining whether or not I was valuable as a person. The code began to destroy the very fabric of our family!

To resolve this dilemma, I began to dictate "The Rules" the girls were expected to follow whenever we were together in public. As Bruce Willis portrayed in the movie *The Kid*, I became an image consultant. They were expected to project our family's perfection to the world. You can imagine the unbelievable pressure this put on our daughters. Not only did **they** need to seem "perfect", they needed to reflect **my** perfection as well! I was so blind. I had convinced myself that we were just being great parents doing what we had to do in order to raise great kids. Self-deception is a powerful force.

The foolishness of this strategy was exposed when April, our youngest, was five years old. We decided to take the girls on vacation to Lancaster, Pennsylvania's Amish country. The girls loved horses and we thought they would really enjoy seeing the horse-drawn buggies. Upon arrival, we went to the hotel where we expected to get a room. The owner of the hotel informed us that he didn't have a room available that was large enough to accommodate our family. However, he recommended that we go across the road, to a Mennonite family who owned a large house and often rented out a part of it. So, across the road we went.

The family had six children, three of them the same ages as our girls. Within a few minutes after meeting them, I sensed that they were everything we should be but weren't: PERFECT! Later I realized the untruth of this, but that was the conclusion I hastily formed that day. My stress-level went through the roof! I developed an instant migraine. We rented the room, but all I wanted to do was keep the girls isolated so this family wouldn't discover what miserable failures we were as parents.

For three hours, my plan of isolation seemed to be working like a charm until my headache became so brutal I knew I had to lie down. Bob wanted to go for a walk and since I wasn't feeling up to it, I suggested he go alone while the girls and I stayed behind. Soon after, I heard a soft knock on the door to our suite. It was one of the Mennonite daughters asking if my girls could come out to play with them. My children were super excited about the proposition. *OH NO*, I thought! Sarah, I knew, wouldn't be a problem, as this was a new environment, and she was still amenable—for the most part—to playing the "image game." Jamie wouldn't be a problem, being very compliant and well-behaved. It was April I was worried about. She was strong-willed, having the energy of three children, and always getting into some kind of trouble.

As I didn't want them outside and mingling with these "perfect" children, I initially said no. It wasn't long before my headache was almost unbearable, so I relented. I sat on the edge of the bed and beckoned April over. Cupping my hand gently under her chin, I raised her head to eye level: "Okay, I'm going to let you guys go out and play with these children, but you can only stay out there for fifteen minutes!" April nodded in agreement, as did the other two, in spite of their disappointment. I had chosen fifteen minutes because I truly believed that April could stay out of trouble for that short amount of time.

I tipped April's head up a little higher and bore my eyes into hers, intentionally leaning closer to her face: "April, I want you to be a good girl out there and behave. Do you understand?" She nodded. I added, "And if you do anything to misbehave or embarrass me, I will kill you. Do you understand?" I could see a look of terror come in her eyes, which was the response I was hoping for. Once again, she nodded. Of course I had no intention to follow through on this deadly threat, but the fact that I would even resort to this type of behavior clearly illustrates how drastically interwoven my self-worth was with their behavior.

EMBARRASSED—WHAT WILL THEY THINK?

The girls headed outside for their fifteen minute play-date and I laid down to close my eyes. I immediately fell asleep, and I am sure I slept LONGER than fifteen minutes! I was awakened by a gentle knock on the door once again. This time it was one of the family's older teenage girls, "Excuse me, Mrs. Gregory, but April was in the emu's pen with my little brother. They were chasing the emu and throwing rocks at it. I assumed you wouldn't want her doing that, because emu's can be dangerous, so I told them both to get out of the pen. I just thought you would want to know." I was mortified! My greatest fear had been realized, and I was immediately flooded with shame, worthlessness and embarrassment. Anger was in the mix as well. I had no time to recover from this onslaught of emotions when the other door opened and in bounded April. She had always loved adventure and excitement and this emu-chasing escapade was right up her alley. I asked her, "What were you thinking?!?" "It was fun, Mommy!" Oh brother, where do you go with this? When Bob got back to our room I told him of April's antics. There was a part of it that was funny, no doubt. However, my image of "perfection" was quickly crumbling at my feet, along with my self-worth.

We recovered from this embarrassing episode and eventually became very good friends with this family. To avoid ever experiencing similar embarrassment, I re-doubled my efforts at "image-managing" our children, and everyone tried to settle into their "expected roles." Although the girls had plenty of rules and regulations to live by, it was apparent that there was a critical part missing: the healthy, unconditional love that we had seen openly displayed in many families was absent in ours. Unfortunately, because of our own insecurities, Bob and I had modeled an extremely conditional love to our girls. We began to see it for what it was and wanted off the hamster wheel. However, this paradigm shift seemed insurmountable because we had not let God deal with our spirit of pride. We were trying to alter our behavior without putting our hearts on His altar. As a result, although we desired to parent differently, very little actually changed. We still attempted to maintain an image of the perfect family. An implosion was imminent.

Bob and I were perfectly poised to learn first-hand the wisdom in the expression, "Rules without relationship leads to rebellion." Our family facade publicly crashed five years later, when Sarah outwardly rebelled and our family unit was exposed for what it really was ... a sham. In hind-sight, I am so incredibly thankful that God used Sarah as an agent for her parents' exposure. However, at the time, it was very painful; not just for Bob and I, but for Sarah as well.

NOWHERE TO HIDE

Sarah had always been strong-willed, and although she had reluctantly been complying with our demands for many years, she had finally reached her limit. Sarah finished high school when she was sixteen, and then attended bible college in western New York State for one year. Bob and I were elated. Not only were we thrilled that she was interested in pursuing her faith, but it also reinforced the image we wanted to portray. Sarah had been struggling personally with her faith, and we were hoping this opportunity would help her sort things out. I look back now and realize why she was struggling with her faith—she lived with hypocrisy on a daily basis! After a year of Bible school, she left for India for three months, to do missionary work. We thought things were headed in a very positive direction. However, to our surprise, within a year of returning, Sarah proclaimed herself to be an agnostic.

We were crushed. To make matters worse, she threw off all the restraints that our rules and "religion" had placed upon her. She decided that she was going to live with integrity. She was not going to behave one way while believing another. Although it was not the path we were hoping for, in hind-sight, I applaud her integrity. Later, through a set of circumstances that were very painful for all involved, she ended up moving in with her boyfriend.

As a result, there was no more hiding behind our facade. She was living in our small community, and as much as I wanted to protect my pride, it was impossible. Bob and I were devastated and heartbroken. I would like to say that we were only devastated and heartbroken for Sarah and her situation, but that would be a lie. Sarah's actions broadcasted to the world what we had always known in our hearts: we were a broken family; anything but perfect. We were deeply affected and totally embarrassed by the public exposure. We were parental failures wearing cloaks of shame.

Our initial response was to try and justify ourselves. Thankfully, God quickly changed our focus from what <u>Sarah</u> was doing to what <u>we</u> had done to facilitate such behavior. God started breaking down our defenses. He led us to look within and it was not pretty! Bob and I began a new season that was both life-changing and devastating at the same time. Finally recognizing (and admitting) that Sarah's actions had more to do with us than her "rebellion", I remember thinking *"If we can just figure out where this mess first started, maybe we can FIX it!"* Thus began months of torment: sleepless nights, reliving our parenting "play-by-play," attempting to pinpoint where and how we had gone off track.

We were clueless. All we knew was that something had gone terribly amiss. Neither of us confided in the other that we both were lost in the same mental-maze. It would be months later before we would discover that. I remember sorting through one memory after another, advancing chronologically, trying to isolate the **one single event** that destroyed our family. Independently, Bob and I were convinced that if we could identify this event, we would be able to put an end to the craziness. Little did we realize that what we were reaping was not the result of a single *event*, but rather a life-long pattern.

One day, exhausted and disheartened, we finally admitted our frustration to each other, and were shocked to realize we had been walking the same discouraging journey. As we talked and shared, we admitted what had been a nagging suspicion in each of our hearts: we <u>had</u> found the enemy, and it was **us**! We saw our parenting style for what it really was and were devastated. What we had once been so blind to now seemed so obvious. We were guilty of ruling with an authoritarian style of parenting in order to protect ourselves and to project a false image. When God showed us the ugliness of our actions, it absolutely broke our hearts. We cried and repented, and gave God permission to do a deep work in this area. The hypocritical facade we had created was now fully exposed to all that knew us. Sarah's actions spoke volumes.

TIME TO OWN IT

Where to start with reversing all the ugliness God had shown us? Once again, we admitted we were clueless. How could we make practical changes in our parenting style? Sarah was now eighteen years old and no long living in our house. We had lost that opportunity ... it was disheartening. However, Jamie and April were fourteen and twelve, respectively, and we determined not to continue to be the parents Sarah had known for her entire life. The first thing Bob and I did was take ownership of our failures. It would have been easy to cast Sarah as the villain and blame her. However, that was not the truth and we vowed not to live in that "valley of death" any longer! Sarah was responsible for her own actions and although we felt she was making some life choices that would later cost her dearly, we also knew that she was not the only one at fault.

We started exposing the truth about the hypocrites we had been behind closed doors to others! It was embarrassing, but to tell you the truth, by that time we were so broken and humbled that the personal cost to us seemed insignificant. We were tired of existing in this self-imposed prison, and we determined to do whatever it took to free ourselves and our girls! I imagine some people were shocked when they learned what type of parents we had truly been, just as I'm certain there were others who were not.

Honestly, God had made such a significant change in our hearts that we really didn't care anymore what anyone thought. We just wanted freedom! We dismantled the image we had painstakingly crafted over so many years and decided to let people see us for who we really were. Gone was the protective fortress we had constructed. Instead, we would now live in a "glass house," revealing the good, the bad, and the ugly—the "real" us to the world! It was one of the best decisions we ever made.

The pressure we had imposed on Jamie and April began to dissipate. We freed them to be themselves. For the first time in their lives, our daughters knew they would be loved and accepted regardless of their actions. However, especially for Jamie, the "perfect performance" was very hard to shed as she felt a responsibility to protect us from further hurt and disappointment. Slowly, our family dynamic was changing in a very real way. The tension that had always been a constant in our house was abating. Joy and laughter gradually emerged and changed the atmosphere. For so many years, Bob and I had only been concerned with adherence to "rules" and "our image." We now realized how empty that is when not coupled with deep relational connections. We prayed it wasn't too late.

Sarah taught us a lesson that forever changed and impacted the dynamic of our family. As painful as it was to go through—to be utterly broken—we were grateful that we were no longer the same parents we had once been. We did not realize how drastically we had changed until nearly five years later when April was seventeen.

April had always been full of energy and ideas, and loved adventures, excitement and fun. However, her definition of excitement and fun was a bit different than ours. She had convinced herself that fun and adventures ended at eighteen and was therefore on a mission to fit a whole life of excitement into her teenage years. There was little that was off-limits to her. I would occasionally tell April that she was like a kite flying high in the sky, flapping in the high winds, while I was standing on the ground holding her very thin string. I was trying to keep her from whipping out of control, but she could ultimately break the string and crash to the ground. I had an awful premonition that I simply could not shake. April was living somewhat recklessly and we were both concerned.

It culminated one evening when she was a few months shy of her eighteenth birthday. She approached me saying she thought she might be pregnant, asking for my thoughts regarding what she should do. My heart sank. I asked her if she had taken a pregnancy test? She had not. She said she was going to go to the store to purchase one.

> WE UNDERSTOOD THAT BEING "LESS THAN PERFECT" DID NOT MAKE ANY OF US LESS VALUABLE.

Later, I saw her come out of the bathroom and asked her to share the result with me. She simply said, "I'm pregnant," and collapsed to the floor. My heart ached for her. I instinctively knew that this would be a road that would either make or break her. I wanted to take the pain and make everything all better, but I knew that was impossible.

Bob and I were now different, having grown over the past five years. The opinion of our community, church and friends no longer acted as the compass by which we guided our lives. We knew that regardless of what it cost us, we would stand with April and our grandchild. The personal cost made little difference. April and her baby were our priority. Our reputation was not. We had been broken, and we had learned humility. Image no longer dictated our actions and we understood that being "less-than-perfect" did not make any of us less valuable. Bob's and my identity were no longer threatened by our children's mistakes. Our priority was to be true to ourselves, our family and to our God. I will forever be thankful that we learned these lessons PRIOR to April getting pregnant. Had her pregnancy occured earlier, we may have sacrificed April and her baby on the altar of our reputations. Instead, we fully embraced April and her unborn baby, choosing to put <u>our reputation</u> on that altar for what we believed would be the final death blow.

I knew this situation would test how deeply the lessons we had previously learned had impacted our hearts. During the ensuing months, there were occasional moments when I would feel shame or embarrassment trying to overpower me. Thoughts of what failures we had been as parents (to have a daughter in a situation like this) would start to lure me down the path of hopelessness. However, very quickly I would see the lie for what it was and stand strong with my daughter. We were committed to April and her journey. We were not going to let self-pity or shame be our focus! April was in a very fragile place and we would do everything within our power to make sure she came out of this situation a stronger woman.

Once the initial shock of the pregnancy lessened, April decided that she most definitely wanted to raise the baby growing within her. Privately, we worked together through issues that ultimately strengthened April's relationship with God. We would counsel her about the change involved with caring for a child. Publicly, we steadfastly stood by her side: we were both her shield and fortress. As Bob and I had years of experience to draw from, we took every opportunity to impart strength and courage to her as well. The journey had its tears, it had its pain, but all in all it was an AMAZING season marked be an abundance of joy, love and acceptance. Bob and I were utterly amazed to see how far we'd come as parents, and we could give thanks to no one other than God.

Slowly, yet consistently, we saw April change as well. She became more confident, brave and determined to stand by the choices she was making. When former friends and peers would convey judgment and rejection, she stood firm. Did it hurt her? Absolutely. However, I believe that knowing her family stood solidly behind her gave her the confidence she needed to feel loved and accepted despite her mistakes.

Many people were watching to see how the situation would unfold. I hadn't fully realized that at first, nor was it my focus. Everyone knew what strict and unforgiving parents we had been and I think many were waiting for the ax to fall. Again, what others thought of us did not matter. We simply focused on what God wanted us to do. How did He want us to proceed? What could we do to facilitate restoration with April and help insure that her baby would be born knowing that he/she was welcomed, wanted and loved? We certainly did not want this child coming into the world bearing shame and embarrassment, feeling inherently damaged. We had never walked this path before, but were determined to do everything we could to position April and her baby for success. The community was watching—offering many differing opinions of what we should be doing—but we focused on what we felt God wanted us to do. Years earlier, we had chosen to live in a glass house and it was now apparent that our decision would prove to be either a blessing or a curse. We still weren't sure which.

Transparency proved to be an incredible blessing. To our surprise, many of the Christians we were associated with chose to embrace April and her unborn baby. They loved, accepted, encouraged and spoke life into her and her situation. It was truly a beautiful thing to behold. It was so incredible to see the body of Christ rise to the occasion, offering love and forgiveness. Unfortunately, there were also some well-meaning Christians who brazenly informed us that they did not approve of the way April's pregnancy was being handled.

We did our best to shelter her from their unforgiving judgmental attitude. She was having enough trouble forgiving herself, she didn't need to hear it from others. As the months progressed, there was an obvious restoration that was reflected in April's countenance. It began to impact the community around us. Other young ladies who felt they had fallen from God's grace began to feel a sense of renewed hope. Parents were also being impacted by the unfolding situation, as many had teens and young adults who had also made poor choices. They were encouraged as they witnessed the life, happiness and reconciliation blossoming in our family. People that had lost hope of ever changing were suddenly encouraged.

It wasn't long before others started to thank us for allowing them to witness the miraculous transformation within our family. We were shocked as that had never been our desire or intention. Yet God had a bigger plan other than just rescuing April and her baby, Phoebe. He was using our willingness to live a life of transparency in order to bring restoration to many others. What the enemy could have used for destruction and devastation in our family, God totally redeemed and transformed ... not just in our lives, but in the lives of countless others as well. Had we chosen to retreat under a cloud of shame, the story would have unfolded very differently. Letting the world see the real us beamed a beacon of light into an otherwise dark situation. It yielded abundant life and the benefits far exceeded the risk!

KEY #5—PARTNERING WITH GOD IS A CHOICE

I am convinced that the single most important reason for April experiencing success and freedom in a situation that could have devastated her, is that Bob and I were able to freely partner with God to help her experience the Father's love. Since our identity was no longer intertwined with the behavior of our children, we were free to love her as agents of healing and restoration. It would have been impossible had we not first allowed God to do the deep work in our hearts. The well-being of April and Phoebe was our only focus. We were determined to do whatever we felt was in the heart of Father God; the fear of man no longer held any sway over us.

Today Phoebe is nine years old and an amazing young lady! She is full of passion and joy and has a personal relationship with Jesus. To know her is to love her. April and Phoebe lived with Bob and me for the first five years of her life. April attended college, graduated and has a great job. Two years ago April married a Christian man who loves Phoebe as his own. God is a God of "second-chances" and a God of restoration: such a beautiful thing to behold and experience!

PRAYER FOR CHOOSING TO PARENT WITHOUT AN IDENTITY CRISIS

Heavenly Father, I admit that it is so easy to have my identity entwined with the behavior of my children and those in relationship with me. Sometimes it is so gradual and so deceptive that I don't even see it for what it is. I quiet myself before You, Father, and ask You to identify any areas in my identity that are intertwined with the opinions and actions of others. I ask God that You would come now, as the Great Physician, and begin a surgery to separate any ties that are not of you. I choose to trust You to do this work.

Sometimes, Father, it gets so muddled that I don't even know who I am without others speaking and defining value or identity to me... I realize now that depending on others to speak value to my identity can be a slippery-slope that I do not want to be on. Papa, it is your voice that I want to hear. It is what YOU say about me that matters most! So, Papa, I quiet myself before You and position myself to hear Your voice... what would You like to speak to my heart? Who am I? What was I created for? What do You say about me? Who do You say I am? (Allow God to speak to your heart and write down everything that comes to mind)

Thank You, Father, for Your words of LIFE! Thank You for Your love for me. Thank You that I am significant! That I matter to You... Not for what I can do, but because of who I am!! You love me... Thank You! Father, I ask that You would put deep in my heart the truth that You just shared with me. That You would put it so deep in my heart that no man and no circumstance would ever be able to shake it loose. Regardless of what may happen around me, Your truth will always be my mooring, my anchor.

Papa, I admit that in the past I allowed the actions of others to speak to my identity. I allowed the actions and words of others to determine my worth. I repent for allowing anyone other than You to determine my value. By the power invested in me through Jesus Christ, I now break all association and all power that false identities have held over my life. I now recognize them for what they truly are: a trap and a lie. I choose instead to believe only what You speak to me, Father. I choose to only believe the Truth. By the power invested in me I also choose to break off the people-pleasing spirit and the fear of man. Father, the only one I want to fear is You. I want to love what You love and hate what You hate. Let my life be a pleasing, Living Epistle for You. For this I give You thanks. Amen.

SIX

PERSEVERANCE
CHOOSING NOT TO GIVE UP

*"Many of life's failures are people who did not realize
how close they were to success when they gave up."*

THOMAS EDISON

*"It's not that I'm smart, it's just that I
stay with problems longer."*

ALBERT EINSTEIN

"Age wrinkles the body. Quitting wrinkles the soul."

DOUGLAS MACARTHUR

When I contemplate individuals who have persevered despite overwhelming odds, Winston Churchill immediately comes to mind. Not always popular, and certainly not as polished as some would have liked, Churchill was a man secure in his own convictions and could not be shaken or dissuaded. He was convinced that God had called him as a voice in the restoration and preservation of world peace and no one was going to persuade him otherwise. He often stood alone against what seemed to be an insurmountable task, yet refused to give into discouragement and defeat. He believed he was mandated by God to fulfill this vital role and refused to let this destiny escape his grasp.

The most commonly cited Churchill quote is an excerpt from a speech given at Harrow school: *"... this is the lesson: never give in, never give in, never, never, never—in nothing, great or small, large or petty—never give in except to convictions of honour and good sense. Never yield to force; never yield to the apparently overwhelming might of the enemy ..."* When reading this quote you might assume that Churchill was speaking from the side of victory and success. However, that was not the context for this speech. This speech was delivered on October 29, 1941, in the very midst of heated battle! Churchill hadn't achieved any victory at all when he spoke these powerful words. As a matter of fact, the situation seemed very grim and hopeless. World War II began on September 1939, and when Churchill uttered these amazing words, Britain—being just an isle—was almost single-handedly trying to withhold Nazi Germany's attempt to take over the world. The future looked dark indeed and although Churchill was sounding the alarm and trying to gather allied forces to Britain's efforts, it would not be until December 7, 1941 that the United States finally engaged.

Knowing this makes Churchill's speech even more remarkable. Even in the midst of what appeared to be a totally hopeless situation, Churchill delivered words that came straight from his heart and impacted generations to come. His words were empowered not only because they were true, but especially because they were his "true-north." He embodied these words; he lived by them and modeled to others how to do the same.

Merriam-Webster defines "persevere" as "to persist in a state, enterprise, or undertaking in spite of counter influences, opposition, or discouragement." Synonyms include: steadfastness, persistence, tenacity, determination, resolve, resolution and staying-power, just to name a few. It is a quality that each of us can possess, yet given a choice, many of us would decline. Innately we realize that perseverance is developed only by trials, and who wants that? Likewise, the truth of Romans 5:3-5 often elicits the same response in our souls, *"And not only that, but we also glory in tribulations, knowing that tribulation produces perseverance; and perseverance, character; and character, hope. Now hope does not disappoint, because the love of God has been poured out in our hearts by the Holy Spirit who was given to us."* Reading that Scripture, we are tempted to forgo the blessings of developed character and hope, if it means we can also avoid trials and hardships.

Winston Churchill, however, did not embrace this mindset. He utilized the tribulation of unrest between the nations to develop inner perseverance, thereby forging his character, resulting in him becoming a prisoner of HOPE. He envisioned a world of peace and this hope became unshakable. He hoped that people—nations—would stand up against the tyrannical evil that was threatening to overtake all of mankind. He foresaw a better future and was driven by that vision. Because he was faithful to his mandate, other countries eventually aligned with his vision and the rest is history. Against all odds, he powerfully exemplified perseverance, which eventually led the world to freedom. His hope had become contagious.

Similarly, I love a particular Anthony Hopkins quote in the movie "The Edge." Lost in the Alaskan wilderness with Alec Baldwin, Hopkins is determined to beat the odds and survive the nightmare, despite the fact that neither possess any survival skills or deep-wilderness training. At one point, when Baldwin becomes bitterly discouraged and wants to give up, Hopkins begins telling him that others have survived similar circumstances, and proclaims, "What one man can do, another can do!" Baldwin is reluctant to agree, so Hopkins demands that Baldwin repeat the statement after him, over and over, until they are both yelling it with great conviction. You can actually see belief and encouragement begin to envelop Baldwin as he shouts the mantra. I love that portion of the movie because as I watch them proclaim the truth, a deep sense of hope and courage grips my soul as well. Innately, I know those words are true. If one man (or woman) can do it, so can another! Often, the difference between success and failure is simply perseverance. Winston Churchill exhibited that in a powerful way!

PERSEVERANCE MUST BE DEVELOPED, IT CANNOT BE GIVEN

I believe there are two basic reasons we don't experience more perseverance in our own lives or see it in those around us. The first being most individuals don't possess a vision for their lives that is greater than themselves. The second is that perseverance usually emerges from the depths of a testing or trial and we all hate those! I'll never forget God expanding Bob's and my life vision and turning our world upside-down! It was the very first time that we led an MMI group, and one of the weeks was titled "Faith Vision and Trust." The homework for that week was to ask God to reveal His vision for your spouse, and then His vision for the "one-flesh" marriage relationship.

By week's end, Bob and I had received answers to our prayers. The modalities God used were unique to each of us, but their mandates were nearly identical. I was nearing the end of the week of prayer when God surprisingly gave me a vision. This was not the manner in which God usually spoke to me: so it surprised me and got my undivided attention! In the vision I was standing in a large field atop the hill rising behind our house. As I stood, looking down towards the valley, I heard voices. They were muted at first, but seemed to be growing louder and louder. Suddenly a group of warriors came running up and over the hill, each armed with a shield in one hand and a sword in the other. They were obviously on a mission! To my surprise, I saw that Bob was leading the army! Running ahead of them, he periodically spun around, waving his sword in the air, and shouted encouragement to those who followed.

Immediately I was reminded of Joshua Lawrence Chamberlain, an officer for the Federal Army during the Civil War. Prior to the war, Chamberlain was a professor of languages and rhetoric at Bowdoin College in Maine. The outbreak of the war deeply bothered Chamberlain and he wanted to actively serve his country. He volunteered and became a Lieutenant Colonel of the newly formed 20th Maine regiment. Although present at several other battles, it would be the Battle of Gettysburg that would make Chamberlain a legend, resulting in him being awarded the medal of Honor for "conspicuous gallantry." The heroic actions of Chamberlain and the 20th Main regiment are beautifully portrayed in the movie "Gettysburg."

Chamberlain and his troops were posted on the extreme left of the Federal line at Little Round Top. They were commissioned with the seemingly impossible task of holding their position against the onslaught of Confederate General John B. Hood's attack on the Union flank. Holding this position was incredibly vital, for if Hood's men were allowed to flank Chamberlain's 20th Maine, the Confederates would gain access to the back of the Union line, thereby enabling them to attack both front and rear of the line, essentially guaranteeing the victory. Out-gunned and out-numbered, Chamberlain sent an urgent request for reinforcements. He received word that reinforcements were not available. He and his men were solely responsible for holding the line. The fighting was intense. The 20th Maine eventually ran out of ammunition. Defeat seemed inevitable.

The next event is powerfully depicted in the movie. In a moment of desperation, Chamberlain's true courage burst forth. He shouted the order, "Bayonets!" and immediately the men fixed their bayonets to the ends of the rifles. His next order was equally shocking, "Charge!" Charging downhill into the very face of death, Chamberlain led, all the while imparting encouragement to his men. Despite all odds, the Union regiment won the battle, solidifying the Union's victory at Gettysburg, and possibly even the entire Civil War.

In my vision, Bob was fortifying the army behind him, calling them to be courageous and steadfast, just as Chamberlain had done at Gettysburg.

I was shocked; I had never previously viewed Bob in that light. It was a major paradigm shift for me. I spent the next few days pondering what I had seen, not sharing the experience, as I didn't yet fully understand its interpretation. Within days, God clarified that one of Bob's greatest life purposes is to set people free, and that he would be in charge of an "army" that would make a huge impact! In addition, I felt certain that this would not be Bob's purpose alone, but as a "one-flesh" team, it would include both of us.

VISION HOLDS YOU WHEN THINGS GET TOUGH

During that week, Bob received a similar directive as he sought God for our mutual vision and purpose. He'd received a vision as well, although very different from mine. He saw a prison camp with bamboo huts scattered around the outskirts. A single man occupied each hut. The huts were only a bit larger than man-size, and it was obvious to Bob that they were instruments of not just confinement, but torture as well. God then spoke clearly to him and said that his purpose was to "go behind enemy lines and set the captives free." Although knowing this could be very dangerous and required courage, it spoke to a deeper sense of purpose and longing within Bob's heart. He readily agreed to partner with God in this mandate. He had pondered this vision for several days before sharing it with me, wanting to be certain of its meaning. When he finally did share it with me, he was convinced that it was not just HIS calling, but OUR calling.

These two visions, although different in some aspects, were quite similar. We were excited not only to have heard from God, but also because He had given us an assignment that was perfectly-aligned with our personalities! Bob and I had always loved adventures. Coupled with that, nothing pleased us more than helping people escape their inner-prisons to fulfill their God-given purposes and destinies! It seemed

God had considered our individual passions and prepared the perfect assignment for us!

Receiving this mandate from God both rocked our world and changed us to the very core. Fundamentally, it was obvious that this assignment was bigger than anything we could possibly accomplish in our own strength. We knew that without God's help and protection, we would both end up as prisoners, just like the ones we were helping to free. Although we possessed the desire, we didn't have the skill or training necessary to accomplish this task. We instinctively understood that this assignment required maturity on a whole new level! As a result, we undertook several changes in our lives. We began to focus on the type of "tools and training" that would facilitate setting captives free. Our hunger for learning grew exponentially. God was orchestrating our learning curve, and He continually put us in contact with individuals and ministries that propelled us forward. Many years have passed since we first received this calling from God, yet we still continue to learn and grow. Our passion to see people set free never seems to diminish.

> RECEIVING GOD'S MANDATE ROCKED OUR WORLD AND CHANGED US TO OUR VERY CORE.

Without a doubt, the most critical change that Bob and I experienced in accepting our visionary call was in our attitude regarding trials and hardships. Prov. 29:18a says, *"Where there is no vision, the people perish"* (KJV). When faced with hardships or trials, it is very tempting to give up and lose hope if you do not have a specific purpose propelling you forward. It is human nature to desire personal comfort, thus avoiding all trials and tribulations becomes our focus. This is a form of perishing. John C. Maxwell says, *"People change when they hurt enough they have to change, they learn enough they want to change, or they receive enough they are able to change."*

We had learned enough that we wanted to change! God's vision and purpose for us yielded a bigger "yes" than we had previously offered to Him. When faced with trails, we kept the mandate ever-present in the forefront of our minds, causing us to evaluate our lives and decisions differently. Instead of pouring all of our energy into trying to avoid or escape trials, we inwardly said "yes" to the process, knowing that as we embrace it, stronger character traits will develop, rendering us far more effective in our ministry. Our vision became our "true north." We realized that each choice mattered and that God had instilled in us the potential to make a difference to all we met. If we chose to quit or become discouraged it would not only impact us, but also the many others we were called to help. We're not autonomous, we are intimately connected to those around us. First Cor. 12:12-27 says:

> "For as the body is one and has many members, but all the members of that one body, being many, are one body, so also is Christ. For by one Spirit, we were all baptized into one body–whether Jews or Greeks–whether slaves or free–and have been made to drink into one Spirit. For in fact the body is not one member but many. If the foot should say, 'Because I am not a hand, I am not of the body,' is it therefore not of the body? And if the ear should say, 'Because I am not an eye, I am not of the body,' is it therefore not of the body? If the whole body were an eye, where would be the hearing? If the whole were hearing, where would be the smelling? But now God has set the members, each one of them, in the body just as He pleased. And if they were all one member, where would the body be? But now indeed there are many members, yet one body. And the eye cannot say to the hand, 'I have no

need of you'; nor again the head to the feet, 'I have no need of you.' No, much rather, those members of the body which seem to be weaker are necessary. And those members of the body which we think to be less honorable, on these we bestow greater honor; and our unpresentable parts have greater modesty, but our presentable parts have no need. But God composed the body, having given greater honor to that part which lacks it, that there should be no schism in the body, but that the members should have the same care for one another. And if one member suffers, all the members suffer with it; or if one member is honored, all the members rejoice with it. Now you are the body of Christ, and members individually."

We are interrelated. Each one of us matters. Whether or not we fulfill our individual destinies impacts the rest of the Body of Christ!

KEY #6—PROGRESSION TOWARD YOUR VISION IS A CHOICE

As this truth crystallized for us, it began to change the way we approached trials and tribulations. Realizing that our actions truly do impact others caused us to re-evaluate our response to discouragement. Giving in and giving up were no longer options once we had internalized God's vision. Perseverance was the only rational course of action. Ever so slowly, God began to instill perseverance into our characters. Each time we faced a trial, we would deliberately **choose** to progress toward our vision, to not give up, to not lose hope. The more we exercised perseverance, the more it became second nature. After a period of time, it became a habit. Finally, it became part of our identities. We were determined to be faithful to God and to our calling; nothing would be allowed to hinder that. Yes, it even became part of our characters. It wasn't that we had engineered a master plan to achieve this, but it was the vision of our future God had given us that propelled us forward. The earthly problems we encountered dimmed in comparison to the light of our calling.

That is, until five years ago, when I was diagnosed with ovarian cancer and our lives were suddenly turned upside-down. Everything now seemed hopeless and futile. There seemed to be no future to fight for, no vision to spur us on. We found ourselves drowning in the depths of despair. For two weeks after receiving the diagnosis, Bob and I did nothing but cry. Literally. Hopelessness was a shroud we could not escape. It seemed the prayers we sent up were rebounding off the ceiling right back to us. God could not be found. Finally, exhausted and discouraged, we were at the point of throwing in the towel ... giving up.

That was when the most remarkable miracle began to unfold. The Body of Christ came to our rescue and did for us what we could not do for ourselves. By this time in our journey, we had accrued several serious offenses toward the "church." We had been serving God for several decades and it had resulted in plenty of opportunities to become offended. We loved God, but no longer fully trusted His Body. God was about to use this cancer journey to realign our attitudes and heal our hearts.

Immediately, the Body of Christ began to minister to our needs and envelop us in His love. The Lord's "hands and feet" brought in meals, prayed for us, stroked my hair, rubbed my feet, cleaned the house, helped us financially, cried with us and accompanied us to doctors appointments. The acts of kindness were endless. These people manifested "God-in-the-flesh" to us. They offered and embodied the love we so desperately needed. For six months I was so weak I could not attend church. However, during that time, we never once felt lonely or isolated! People would visit almost every day. Bob took six months off of work to care for me, and during that time the Body of Christ blessed us financially enabling him to do so.

Bob and I soon established a daily pattern. He would prepare lunch, go out to the mailbox to retrieve the day's mail and then call me to the table. He usually finished lunch first, as I often picked at my food with little appetite. As I finished my meal, he would open the cards and read each one of them aloud. Often, his voice would break with emotion and tears would spill from our eyes. The love lavished upon us seemed to be more than we could contain. It was as if God knew how important those words of affirmation and love would be in facilitating our healing, as there was **never** a day that we didn't receive at least one card in the mail. We treasured each card (I actually still have every one of them) and the words of life that flowed from them began to change us.

Bob and I had never been recipients of such extravagant love! During my recovery, it was common for people to travel from many miles away in order to encourage and pray for us. It seemed this love towards us had no bounds! It was truly overwhelming and humbling. We couldn't deny it, the Body of Christ is an amazing, living entity! Every person that God used felt like a literal extension of His hand. How could we have taken offense against such a beautiful creature?!? We realized we couldn't. We repented to God for the way we had so wrongly judged the Body of Christ and had allowed our hearts to be hardened toward His church. God used people to lavish His loving heart upon us, and we couldn't help but fall in love with the church all over again!

With our hearts no longer wounded, God began using His church to rescue us. Regardless of whether it was a card, a concerned phone call or a loving visit, a similar theme soon emerged. Individuals began encouraging us by recounting stories of how we had been used by God to make significant changes in their lives. Initially the stories fell on deaf ears, as we felt too hopeless and discouraged to receive them. Gradually, however, it seemed the "spiritual giant" within us began to awaken from its slumber. These people purposely reminded us of who we are, as it seemed we had lost our way during the trauma of the diagnosis, surgery and subsequent treatments. We had lost our vision without any hope of continuing to fulfill it. Relentlessly, God used the love being poured out by His Body to steer us back to our true-north and therefore fully awaken our destiny.

NEVER, NEVER, NEVER GIVE UP!

Bathed in the love and support of friends, a dramatic shift took place within us. Although the doctors had given us a very grim prognosis, we realized that it has **never** been in our nature to roll over and give up! It seemed that a mighty roar was beginning to stir deep within us, waiting and needing to be heard. For many years God had been using trials and tribulations to develop perseverance within us, and we soon realized that perhaps that had been the warm-up, preparing us for this great battle we were currently facing.

Unrelenting tenacity began to re-surface within us, and with it, hope. It's no coincidence that Romans 5:3-5 directly correlates perseverance to hope when it says, *"And not only that, but we also glory in tribulations, knowing that tribulation produces perseverance; and perseverance, character; and character, hope. Now hope does not disappoint, because the love of God has been poured out in our hearts by the Holy Spirit who was given to us."* It seemed only natural to choose the hope offered by God instead of the dire future prophesied by the medical profession. Deut. 30:14-19 says,

"But the word is very near to you, in your mouth and in your heart, that you may do it. See, I have set before you today life and good, death and evil, in that I command you today to love the Lord your God, to walk in His ways, and to keep His commandments, His statutes, and His judgments, that you may live and multiply; and the Lord your God will bless you in the land you go to possess. But if your heart turns away so

you do not hear, and are drawn away, and worship other gods and serve them, I announce to you today that you shall surely perish; you shall not prolong your days in the land which you cross over the Jordan to go and possess. I call heaven and earth as witnesses today against you, that I have set before you life and death, blessing and cursing; therefore choose life, that both you and your descendants may live."

We decided then and there that we were going to choose LIFE and we were going to partner with God to see it happen! I never suspected that allowing God to build perseverance in our character would reap such miraculous benefits.

It has now been more than five years since my initial diagnosis. In countless ways it has been THE most incredible journey that Bob and I have ever embarked upon. There have been times of discouragement —even set-backs—but they are temporary. We immediately bring our focus back to God and LIFE. It has been such an incredible season of growth for both of us! 1 Peter 1:7 says, *"That the genuineness of your faith, being much more precious than gold that perishes, though it is tested by fire, may be found to praise, honor and glory at the revelation of Jesus Christ."* Likewise, Second Cor. 4:17 says, *"For our light affliction, which is but for a moment, is working for us a far more exceeding and eternal weight of glory."* Of course, there are times when our troubles seem anything but "light and momentary," but this journey has grounded us in our faith and in the Word of God like little else ever could have. Bob and I possess a measure of faith we had never dreamed possible. We've experienced exponential growth and we wouldn't trade this for anything in the world!

I chose to discontinue all cancer treatments two years ago when the doctors told us there was nothing more to be done to significantly prolong my life. Realizing that God is my only hope, I began to grow and change in ways that I had always desired, but never quite knew how to achieve.

REALIZING THAT GOD IS MY ONLY HOPE, I BEGAN TO GROW AND CHANGE IN WAYS THAT I HAD ALWAYS DESIRED BUT NEVER QUITE KNEW HOW TO ACHIEVE.

I decided to investigate whether God's desire was to heal me or not. A friend gave me a copy of T.L. Osborn's book *Healing the Sick* and it rocked my world! The book is chock-full of Scriptures proving God's heart is **always** towards healing. Although I had read the Bible cover-to-cover numerous times, I decided I was going to reread it, this time with a different purpose. I was going to read the Bible as if I had never read it before, deliberately ignoring the various biblical interpretations and theologies I had been taught over the years by different denominations. If God's Word said it, I was going to believe it! It was going to be as simple as that. It proved to be one of the best decisions I have ever made. The Scriptures once again became alive and exciting! So much truth was right there before my eyes, yet I had always come up with reasons or excuses to explain why miracles were no longer readily seen today. If God's Word said it, that was evidence enough. It has resulted in the most exciting God-journey I have ever experienced.

My faith has grown in ways that I once thought was impossible!. Romans 4:17b-18a speaking of Abraham says, *"'I have made you the father of many nations.' He is our example and father, for in God's presence he believed God can raise the dead and call into being things that don't even exist yet. Against all odds, when it looked hopeless, Abraham believed the promise and expected God to fulfill it. He took God at His word, and as a result he became the father of many nations"* (TPT).

I now understand "against all odds, when it looked hopeless ... he believed the promise and expected God to fulfill it. He took God at His word ..." in a whole new way. Despite everything the medical profession has predicted, I am fully hoping and expecting to live a long and healthy life! I have already outlived my oncologist's dire prediction by one year! I am not in any way implying that someone should not seek medical help, or stop the medical regimen they are currently following! For me it was somewhat of an easy decision. My oncologist ordered another round of chemotherapy, predicting it would only prolong my life by six months. If you have ever done chemotherapy, or have known someone who has, you realize that you are usually quite sick from the side-effects for those six months. Therefore, I did not consider it to be an option for me. Honestly, if a new and effective treatment for ovarian cancer was developed (such as immunotherapy) which resulted in minimal side-effects, I would most certainly consider it. Otherwise, God truly is my only hope.

I told my oncologist I have decided to put all my eggs in one basket ... that basket is God. He is my greatest hope and best bet. I have been a Christian for thirty-five years. I only wish I had learned of God's deep love for His children and all He gives us access to through the New Covenant (made available through the blood of Christ) sooner. Regardless, my attitude is "better late than never!"

INTIMACY GROWS THROUGH THE JOURNEY

I imagine there are some individuals who are expecting me to die, but that doesn't upset or discourage me. If I die, I die ... but if I live it is because God's Word is true! Earlier on in this journey, while I was still very weak and recuperating from the surgery, God imparted two very specific directives. The first is from Ps. 118:17, *"I shall not die, but live, and declare the works of the Lord."* Secondly, He told me that this journey would be a "Job experience" for me. Upon hearing that this journey was going to be a "Job experience", I was not initially reassured. However, after meditating on it for several years, I have now come to realize Job's intimacy with God grew exponentially because of his journey! All Job initially lost was eventually returned to him ... with compounded interest!

Bob and I have taken very specific steps to partner with God in the healing process, although I realize that I am incapable of healing myself—only He can do that. Jesus was beaten, tortured and crucified on the cross so that we could partake of His finished work: complete salvation (body, soul and spirit)! I am not responsible for making God's Word come to pass... He is and He is fully able and willing to do so! We can, however, choose not to partner with Him and His Word, which would be a tragedy. The first and most important step we undertook in this partnership with God was to actually believe His Word! If the Bible says it, that is good enough for me! I believe His word is infallible, and if it is in the Bible I can trust it (despite the teachings of various denominations and sects).

That principle alone has totally transformed our walk with God from a mundane duty into an exciting adventure! The second critical step forward on this path was to invite our "community" to join us on this journey. We have continued to remain very transparent and vulnerable, allowing others to minister hope, encouragement and practical help to us when needed. When you embark on a journey like this it is nearly impossible to succeed in an isolated vacuum. Inevitably, there will be times of discouragement and fatigue. It is vital to have community surrounding you; to "hold hope" when you lose it and to get you back on track when you've been derailed. It's very easy to isolate yourself when going through trials, yet critical to not do so.

I realize there are many who have believed in God's healing, yet were not healed. Do I understand that? Of course not! (I hope someday to make some sense of that mystery.) I do know that God's Word promises healing and that Christ suffered on the cross to set us free from all disease, sickness and infirmity. Although I believe it is the Father's heart to heal His children, it is clearly not being manifested on earth as consistently as it should be. Until then, Christians have a win-win! If we receive our physical healing while here on earth we win: if we graduate into the heavenly realm, we also win. The Passion Translation summarizes it beautifully in Philippians 1:20-21, *"No matter what, I will continue to hope and passionately cling to Christ, so that he will be openly revealed through me before everyone's eyes. So I will not be ashamed! In my life or in my death, Christ will be magnified in me. My true life is in the Anointed One, and dying means gaining more of him."*

In the past several years, I have been greatly encouraged as I've witnessed a major and dramatic shift happening in the Body of Christ! It's apparent that God is re-awakening His Bride to the supernatural power and love that we were created to carry on earth! It has become apparent that God is ushering in an era of miraculous signs, wonders and healings. Whereas in previous times it was unusual to hear of God miraculously healing or raising someone from the dead (and when you did hear of it, the stories always seemed to originate from a third-world country!), it is becoming more common to hear of miracles occurring closer to home. On a weekly basis, individuals are being miraculously healed of terminal or life-limiting diseases, as well as being raised from the dead, with medical records to substantiate it! I believe this kind of report will soon be the "norm" rather than the "exception"!

As Believers, we are living in a very exciting time. Although similar opportunities were readily available to the early church, throughout the history of Christianity the working of signs and miracles was limited to a select few. It is now be presented and offered to us all! God is holding out his scepter and inviting us to partner with Him in this new era of ushering in the miraculous.

You would expect the Body of Christ to be jumping at this opportunity! Instead, we are witnessing quite the opposite. Many religious churches and leaders have stubbornly risen up against what God is ushering in, accusing it of being fueled by the demonic. Although I believe this conclusion is driven solely by fear, it is rendering a large portion of the body impotent. Similarly, I believe we are not seeing the Body of Christ consistently walking in the miraculous because we are not believing in the power of Jesus' Name. In Ephesians 1:21, when speaking of Christ it says, *"Far above all principality and power and might and dominion, and every name that is named, not only in this age but also in that which is to come."* Again, in Philippians 2:9, it says of Jesus, *"Therefore God also highly exalted Him and given Him the name which is above every name."*

NO OTHER NAME

When Jesus was raised from the dead, He imparted his authority to us (his Body) along with the privilege of ministering in His name! Although we may understand that intellectually, we have not accepted it as reality in our hearts. Why am I saying this? Because I lived like that for most of my Christian life. If you had asked me if I believe the name of Jesus is greater than any other name, I would have emphatically answered, "YES!" However, my belief was not manifested in my lifestyle. I did not have the confidence to pray for someone to experience the miraculous, regardless of the individual's circumstances. If a person approached me for prayer, to be healed of cancer, I immediately cringed, believing the name "cancer" to be greater than the name "Jesus"! Parkinson's disease? Greater than the name of Jesus! Lou Gehrig's disease? Greater than the name of Jesus! Cerebral Palsy? Greater than the name of Jesus! Physical deformities? You get the idea. The list went on and on ... Once you allow your faith to be eroded by a false belief-system, there is no end in sight.

However, the truth is that Jesus' name IS greater than ALL diseases, greater than ALL circumstances! I now understand that, and most importantly, believe it in my heart! God is looking for a believer that will actually <u>believe</u> Him. He is holding out His scepter, inviting us to partner with Him in these exciting times! Will you join Him or will you choose to be a side-line observer with a critical attitude? We each must decide how to answer that question. Bob and I have whole-heartedly jumped in! We dare you to join us. The best is yet to come!

In summary, two keys have truly helped Bob and me navigate this journey towards healing. The first—experiencing and treasuring "community," which in our case, was provided by the Body of Christ. The continued love and support being lavished upon us creates a "safe-place" atmosphere in which to embrace life and healing. I fully understand the power of community as being critical to reaching our destiny. We were never meant to navigate trials alone. The other key been, without a doubt, perseverance. Years earlier we had purposed to embrace tribulation and hardships, which have resulted in perseverance becoming part of our characters. That led to hope and hope does not disappoint. We all need hope in our lives! I am a prisoner of hope as is Bob. It is a wonderful way to live. We wouldn't want it any other way!

It cannot be said more beautifully than Romans 8:24-25: *"For we were saved in this hope, but hope that is seen is not hope; for why does one still hope for what he sees? But if we hope for what we do not see, we eagerly wait for it with perseverance."*

Perseverance—choosing to not give up—can change our personal histories as well as those affected by our sphere of influence. What if Winston Churchill had not persevered? We would be living in a much darker world. What if Lawrence Chamberlain had believed the obvious: that he and his men were out-gunned, out-numbered and out of ammunition? What if he had not reached deep within and found the courage to persevere? The United States of America would not exist. Perseverance matters although we have to endure trials or hardships in order to attain it. It is well worth it! I encourage you to embrace all that God has for you. He is inviting you on the greatest adventure of your life! Christianity was never meant to be a spectator sport! He is looking for those who will partner with Him, bringing heaven down to earth. Don't shrink back. He wouldn't have called you if He didn't know you were capable! Jump in! Someday, it may make the difference between life and death for you or someone you love.

PRAYER FOR CHOOSING TO PERSEVERE AND NOT GIVE UP

Heavenly Father, I come to You, realizing that Your ways are not always our ways … You always have our best interest and character in mind, whereas we sometimes are willing to sacrifice that to "find the easy way out." That attitude doesn't benefit anyone: not me, and not anyone around me. Perhaps the real issue is that I am reluctant to truly trust You with my life and future … Father, I repent for that attitude; I ask for Your forgiveness. I want to make a difference in this world, and I know that is Your heart for me as well. Today I choose to wholly yield myself to You. Is there anything You would like to speak to my heart, Father?

God, would you speak to me afresh and share Your heart and dreams with me concerning my destiny? Would You speak to me in a very special and unique way? I want to know the specific purpose and mandate that You have reserved for me as my own adventure. What have You specifically created me to do, Father? I want to partner with You; I want to be instrumental in bringing heaven down to earth! I want to make a difference! Share that vision with me, Father, and ignite the fire within!

I realize that nothing worthwhile is ever accomplished without perseverance. Father, although I may never have prayed a prayer like this before, I choose to trust You and ask You to build perseverance in my character. I know I can trust You. You love me more than I love myself, and I know I can trust

You to choose what is best for me. I want my life to matter; I want it to make a difference in the world. I want to have the character of Jesus. I yield my life to You. Let my life bring glory and honor to You!

I also realize that truly great feats require the effort of more than a solitary person. You have put us in "community" for a reason... We need each other. Father, if there are still areas of woundedness in my heart that have kept me from functioning effectively within the community You have placed me in, I ask Your forgiveness. You know my heart, God. You know whether I have been harboring offenses; wearing a mask to protect myself so as to not be vulnerable and transparent. You know, Father, and so do I. I repent for any and all areas which I have not been honoring the blessing of community, and especially the community of family and church. I repent. I choose to turn from the way I have previously behaved and go in a new direction; the direction of Your choosing!

I want to be a person that infectiously spreads LIFE and HOPE everywhere I go! I want to walk in new depths of life, hope, and faith. I know that's Your heart for me as well, so I ask that You would take me by the hand and guide me into the deep waters. I choose to leave the shore of hum-drum safety and trust You in the adventures of a lifetime! I want to be a world-changer, God, and I know that if I partner with YOU it is guaranteed! Each day I choose to partner with You! I love You, Daddy. Amen.

I live my life without regrets.
The choices I make allow me
to live each day in freedom.

CINDA M. GREGORY

LIVING WITHOUT REGRETS

6 ESSENTIAL KEYS TO PERSONAL FREEDOM

If this book has touched you,
I invite you to leave a review on
Amazon so others can find my story.

I would love to hear from you!

cindamgregory@gmail.com